Hong Kong
and Macau

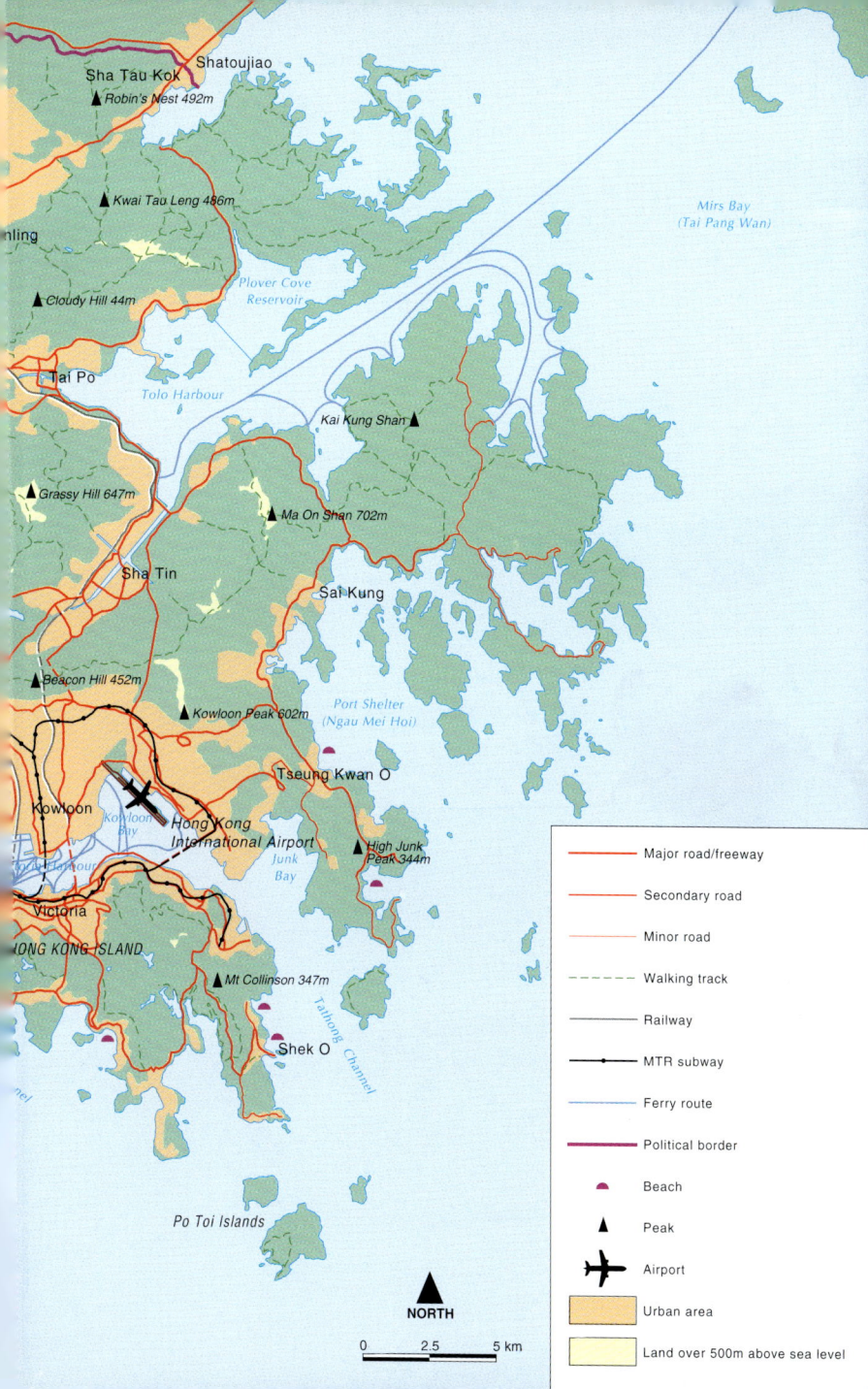

Sha Tau Kok
Shatoujiao
▲ Robin's Nest 492m

▲ Kwai Tau Leng 486m

nling

▲ Cloudy Hill 44m

Plover Cove
Reservoir

Mirs Bay
(Tai Pang Wan)

Tai Po

Tolo Harbour

Kai Kung Shan ▲

▲ Grassy Hill 647m

▲ Ma On Shan 702m

Sha Tin

Sai Kung

▲ Beacon Hill 452m

▲ Kowloon Peak 602m

Port Shelter
(Ngau Mei Hoi)

Tseung Kwan O

Kowloon

Kowloon
Bay

Hong Kong
International Airport

Junk
Bay

High Junk
Peak 344m ▲

Harbour

Victoria

HONG KONG ISLAND

▲ Mt Collinson 347m

Tathong Channel

Shek O

Po Toi Islands

⎯⎯⎯	Major road/freeway
⎯⎯⎯	Secondary road
⎯⎯⎯	Minor road
- - -	Walking track
⎯⎯⎯	Railway
•⎯•⎯•	MTR subway
⎯⎯⎯	Ferry route
⎯⎯⎯	Political border
◗	Beach
▲	Peak
✈	Airport
▬	Urban area
▬	Land over 500m above sea level

▲
NORTH

0   2.5   5 km

Junks sailing past Hong Kong Island

Tin Hau Festival

Hong Kong and Macau

Little Hills Press

Cover Photograph: Reliving Chinese history at the Middle Kingdom.
Back Cover Photgraph: Hong Kong at dusk, from Kowloon peninsula.
©Photographs -Hong Kong Tourist Association, C Burfitt
©Maps - Little Hills Press
Inside front cover map by MAPgraphics, Brisbane.
Text by Fay Smith and Charles Burfitt

Cover by NB Design

Printed in Singapore

Text © Little Hills Press
This edition January 1999
ISBN 1 86315 115 X

Little Hills Press Pty. Ltd.,
37-43 Alexander Street,
Crows Nest NSW 2065
Australia
email: info@littlehills.com
Home Page: http:\\www.littlehills.com

DISCLAIMER

Whilst all care has been taken by the publisher and author to ensure that the information is accurate and up to date, the publisher does not take responsibility for the information published herein. The recommendations are those of the author, and as things get better or worse, places close and others open, some elements in the book may be inaccurate when you get there. Please write and tell us about it so we can update in subsequent editions.

Contents

Hong Kong

(Introduction, History, Climate, Population, Language, Religion, Holidays, Entry Regulations, Exit Regulations, Embassies, Money, Communications, Miscellaneous) 7

Macau

(History, Climate, Population, Language, Religion, Holidays, Entry & Exit Regulations, Money, Communications, Miscellaneous - Travel Information, Tourist Offices) 154

Hong Kong

The special administrative region of Hong Kong lies at the south-eastern tip of China, adjoining the province of Guangdong, and just south of the Tropic of Cancer. The capital of Guangdong is Guangzhou (Canton), and it is 135km (84 miles) north-west of Hong Kong, while Beijing (Peking), the capital of China, is 2000km (1243 miles) to the north.

The total area of Hong Kong is 1070 sq km (413 sq miles), made up of Hong Kong Island, 77.5 sq km (30 sq miles), Kowloon, 12 sq km (5 sq miles), and the New Territories and the 235 islands combined with 980.5 sq km (378 sq miles). The SAR of Hong Kong is roughly 38km (24 miles) from north to south, and 50km (31 miles) from west to east.

The highest mountain is in the New Territories, Tai Mo Shan (958m-3143ft), followed by Lantau Peak (934m-3064ft) on Lantau Island, which is the largest island in the Territory and twice the size of Hong Kong Island.

The better-known mountain, Victoria Peak on Hong Kong Island, is a mere 554m (1817ft).

History

Artefacts discovered by archaeologists on more than twenty sites in Hong Kong indicate there were settlements in Neolithic times. It is thought that in the 2nd millennium BC, people from North China stopped off on their way to Borneo, the Philippines and Taiwan.

The Cantonese began settlements in the area around 100BC, and later came the Hakka, and by the mid-17th century, the Hoklo, who had a reputation for being pirates. At this time Hong Kong was one of the scenes of the last struggles of the Ming dynasty with the newly risen Manchus.

Britain had been trading with China since the late 17th century, with ships arriving from their East India Company bases on the shore of India. Later they were reluctantly allowed to establish a warehouse near Canton to enable them to ship out tea and silk, but they had nothing to trade for these highly desirable goods that appealed to the Chinese. That is, until someone came up with the bright idea of importing opium. It was not long before the whole population was hooked, and the country's silver was being depleted to support the habit.

The Chinese emperor, alarmed by the damage being done to the people and the dwindling silver situation, although not necessarily in that order, declared a ban on opium, and even went so far as to confiscate the British stockpile.

First Opium War

Britain wasn't going to stand for that, so they declared war, and of course won what came to be known as the first Opium War, in 1841. This resulted in a treaty, which incidentally China never recognised, but which forced her to cede Hong Kong Island in perpetuity to the British. The second Opium War, which Britain also won in 1861, saw Kowloon Peninsula and Stonecutters Island become the spoils of war. By 1898 Britain felt the need for more land for defence purposes, but with other wars on her mind at the time, decided on a more peaceful solution and leased the New Territories, including the 235 outlying islands, from China for a period of 99 years. The expiry date, was in 1997.

Now Hong Kong is a Special Administrative Region of China enjoying a high degree of autonomy.

Prior to British occupation, Hong Kong Island had been more or less a fishing village and a haunt of pirates. On January 26, 1841, when Sir J.J. Gordon Bremer planted the first British flag on Hong Kong soil, it was indeed not much more than a "barren rock with hardly a dwelling upon it", as it was described by the then British Foreign Secretary, Lord Palmerston, upon hearing of the realm's newest acquisition.

The settlement didn't have a very rosy beginning either. No sooner had it begun than it was visited by a typhoon, and only five days later, when repairs had begun, another tropical storm brought more devastation. These were followed by fever, fire, and incredibly hot and humid weather, and the population of the recently established burial ground grew by leaps and bounds. Amazingly, so did the number of able-bodied citizens, to the extent that by 1846 the head count was 24,000, and by the turn of the century it had reached 300,000.

The inauguration of the Republic of China in 1911 caused

Hong Kong to become an impartial refuge, for both people and capital. The emergence of nationalism was accompanied by hostility toward foreign interests, and during 1925-27 a boycott excluded British trade from all the ports of South China. This changed, however, after the Japanese conquest of Manchuria, and relations between the British in Hong Kong and Chinese officialdom became increasingly friendly.

Second World War

Hong Kong again became a refuge in 1937 when thousands of Chinese fled from the advancing Japanese. With the outbreak of war in Europe in 1939, the position of the SAR of Hong Kong became precarious, and when the Japanese opened hostilities in December, 1941, they attacked Hong Kong, and the SAR of Hong Kong was surrendered on Christmas Day.

British troops re-entered the city on August 30, 1945, and civil government was re-established in May 1946. The SAR of Hong Kong made a remarkable recovery, but thousands of Chinese returned producing a housing problem, made more acute by the influx of refugees fleeing from the Communist armies in the Chinese civil war, 1948-1950. These refugees included many Shanghai industrialists who were responsible for the birth of Hong Kong's famous textile industry. The population by 1956 had reached 2.5 million.

In December 1966, China accused the British government of allowing Hong Kong to be used by the United States as a base for the Vietnam war.

In May 1967, rioting broke out in Hong Kong and Kowloon following a dispute in a plastic-flower factory in the New Territories. It lasted for several days, and appeared to have been fostered by agitators of the Maoist Communist faction, inspired by China's Cultural Revolution, 1966-69.

Hong Kong's relationship with China has improved, particularly since the death of Mao Tse-tung in 1976, and since China's programme of modernization began in the late 1970s, although it does have a policy whereby illegal immigrants from China are immediately sent back.

The Present

Which brings us back to the present. Talks between Britain and

China began in 1982, and they signed the Sino-British Agreement of 1984. China stated in this that Hong Kong's capitalist lifestyle and social system will be preserved for at least 50 years after 1997, and that it will become a Special Administrative Region, largely self-governing, with the people retaining their property, and the right to travel at will. The existing legal and juridical systems under english Common Law are maintained, ensuring continued recourse to tried and trusted means of litigation and rule of law. The judiciary is independent with the final Court of Appeal based in Hong Kong. English remains the official language and english signage is being maintained. It still maintains its own currency and the administration of Hong Kong is carried out by a Chief Executive who has lived for at least 20 years in the former colony. It must be remembered that Britain only started to give self governing rights to people in Hong Kong in the 1980s and prior to its departure in 1997 it proceeded to dilute the colony of its wealth by building an enormous new airport with most contracts going to British firms. No wonder the administration in Beijing was a little miffed.

Climate

Hong Kong's proximity to the Tropic of Cancer makes it subtropical. Average temperatures are -

Spring (March-May): 21C (70F); humidity 84%.
Summer (May-September): 28C (82F); humidity 83%.
Autumn (September-December): 23C (73F); humidity 73%.
Winter (December-February): 15C (59F); humidity 75%.

The high humidity in Spring is accompanied by fog and rain, and part of Summer (July-September) is the typhoon season, although this does not create any danger because of Hong Kong's very efficient early warning systems. But all in all, the period from October to December is ideal for sightseeing, and the lower humidity makes shopping so much more comfortable.

Population

The population of Hong Kong is around 6.3 million, and it is estimated that 98% of the people are Chinese. The Kowloon Peninsula is home to 2.2 million, Hong Kong Island, 1.3

million, with the remainder living in the New Territories and on the Outlying Islands.

The SAR of Hong Kong is one of the most densely populated areas of the world, with an overall density of approximately 5330 people per sq km.

Language

Cantonese and English are the official languages, and most people in restaurants and shops can speak English. Cantonese is the most widely spoken, although it is apparently a difficult dialect to master as it has nine tones. This means that the one word has nine different meanings, depending on the way it is pronounced.

Nevertheless, if you want to experiment with the language, which may or may not send the locals into fits of laughter, here are some words to get you started.

Good morning - joa san
(they don't say good afternoon or good night.
Goodbye - joygeen.
Thank you (for a service) - m'goi.
Thank you (for a gift) - dorchay.
Shopkeepers often use this when you give them money for a purchase - it doesn't necessarily mean that you could have paid less if you had persevered in the bargaining.
You're welcome - m'sai m'goi
(literally 'it's not necessary to thank').
Never mind - m'gan yu.
(when you can't find anything in a shop that interests you)
Dollar - man.
How much - gay daw cheen.
Very expensive - ho gwai.
Too expensive - tai gwai.
Very cheap - ho peng.

Taxi - dik si.
Straight ahead - jik hui.
Turn left - juen jaw.
Turn right - juen yau.
Stop - teng ni doh.
Go quickly - faai di.

Slow down - maan di.
Hotel - jaudeem.

The menu - tsan pai m'goi.
The bill - m'goi mai dan
Coffee - gar fey
Tea with milk - nai cha
Chinese tea - ching cha
Beer - bar jau
Wine - jau

0	ling		
1	yat		
2	yee		
3	saam	12	sap yee
4	sei	20	yee sap
5	ng	100	baak
6	lok	1000	chin
7	chat	half	boon
8	baat		
9	gau		
10	sap		
11	sap yat		

Places in Hong Kong

Hong Kong - Heung Gong
Kowloon - Gau Lung
New Territories - San Gaai
The Peak - Saan Deng
Central District - Chung Waan
Causeway Bay - Tung Lo Wan
Wanchai - Waan Chai
Tsimshatsui - Kim Sa Jui
Star Ferry, Hong Kong side - Tin Sing Ma Tau
Star Ferry, Kowloon side - Jim Sa Jui Ma Tau
Stanley - Chik Chue
Repulse Bay - Chin Sui Waan
Aberdeen - Heung Gong Chai
Kai Tak Airport - Kai Tak Gei Cheung
Outlying Districts Services Pier - Gong Noy Sin Ma Tau

Macau Ferry Pier - O Moon Ma Tau
Ocean Park - Hoi Yeung Kung Yuen

Religion

The main religion of the residents of Hong Kong is Money, and the main god is the Dollar, but nevertheless there are many temples and churches dedicated to more conventional deities.

The majority of residents are Buddhists, but they seem to have become entwined with Taoists, and others, and in fact some people would not be able to separate the Buddhist gods from the Taoist. For example, one of the most popular Taoist temples, the Wong Tai Sin Temple, has statues of the Buddhist Goddess of Mercy, Kwun Yum, the Taoist civil and martial gods Man and Mo, and one of the Taoist Eight Immortals, Lu Sun Young. And, to cover all bases, within the Wong Tai Sin complex there is a temple dedicated to Confucius.

Buddhism

Buddhism stresses the rejection of materialism and desire, and a sense of harmony with nature. In the 1st century AD, the Emperor Ming-ti sent a delegation to India to learn more about the faith, and when he tried to establish it back home, there was much resistance from the Taoists and the Confucianists. Buddhism received its strongest support from the great Kublai Khan (c 1216-94), who is believed to have built some 42,000 temples, and monasteries for some 215,000 monks.

The Buddhist images most commonly represented include Sakyamuni Buddha (born as Prince Siddhartha in the 6th or 7th century BC), the Healing Buddha (Yeuk See Fat), Kwun Yum (a mortal who became the Goddess of Mercy), and Wen Shu (the God of Wisdom).

Taoism

The oldest religion in China, Taoism was founded by Lao Tzu in 604BC, and his teachings are contained in a book entitled *Tao Te Ching*. In its purist form, Taoism is based on a transcendence of worldly things, stressing harmony with, not dominance over, nature.

Over the years, though, what began as a system of ethics has been altered with the addition of several gods and goddesses, the results of myths and superstitions, and the influence of Buddhism. Every profession or trade has a special god who watches over it, and many homes and shops have shrines at the entrance, with burning joss sticks, or even a piece of fruit, honouring the earth gods.

Among the most popular gods and immortals are: the Jade Emperor, the Supreme Deity of Taoism; Wong Tai Sin, the Healer of Sickness and Teller of Fortunes; Tin Hau, Goddess of Seafarers; and the Eight Immortals, spirits with supernatural powers who each represent a condition of life - poverty, wealth, age, youth, aristocracy, plebianism, masculinity and femininity.

Other objects you may notice are eight-sided mirrors, which reject evil spirits, and paper material objects, such as cars and clothes, which are burned for use by the dead in the afterlife.

Confucianism

The Chinese scholar Confucius (551-479BC) is known to have studied the classic Chinese text *Li Chi*, The Record of Rites, which states, "As the people are taught filial piety and brotherly love at home, with reverence toward the elder and diligent care for the aged in the community, they constitute the way of the king, and it is along this line that states as well families will become peaceful". Basically, this sums up Confucianism, and many families in Hong Kong have ancestral altars in their homes, and pray to the departed in temples. During the Ching Ming and Chung Yeung holidays, everybody visits the graves of their ancestors.

Christianity

Hong Kong has numerous cathedrals and churches of Catholic, Anglican and other denominations, with services in English and Chinese. The teachings of Christianity were brought to Hong Kong by early missionaries who used the port as a base for missions into China, and also by western settlement in the 1800s throughout China itself.

Christmas and Easter are observed, and the private Catholic schools offer some of the finest education available in the city.

Numerous other religious groups, including Sikhs, Hindus, Muslims and Jews, have settled here since the territory was colonised.

Temples

Of the 360 Chinese temples in Hong Kong, most are Buddhist, many are Taoist, and some, known as *miu*, are both. Buddhist temples are usually found in more remote areas which are more conducive to meditation, while Taoist temples are in the urban areas. Although all temples are crowded during festival times, there is no special day for worship, people simply pop in when they feel the need to pay their respects, or seek advice.

The exact position of a temple is determined by *fung shui*. The ideal position is between the spurs of a hill which slope down to the sea, because this is OK with the dragon who lives in the hill. The fact that some of the older temples have had their position changed due to reclamation of land, or the building nearby of skyscrapers, is negated by their original good *fung shui*.

The colourful decoration of the temples has meaning, too. Red means happiness; green stands for peace and eternity; and gold denotes royalty, wealth and strength. The architecture of the roof is important also, and many have ridges of decorative porcelain depicting characters and lucky symbols from Chinese folklore. Green is the traditional colour for the roof, though some of the more modern choose yellow.

There are no restrictions on visiting temples, in fact you will be made to feel welcome, and of course it is expected that you treat them with the same respect that you would show your own church. One small courtesy is appreciated - on entering a temple, it is customary to proceed to the left, around the large cast-iron crock, or *deng*, that holds burning sticks of incense.

There are no entry fees to the temples, but small donations are always gratefully accepted. You can either place money in the box at the entrance or in front of the main altar, or buy some of the incense that is always on sale.

The Chinese Zodiac

Chinese astrology is actually only one element in a very large and complex belief system that includes *fung shui*, numerology, magic and the Chinese almanac. The Zodiac system commands a certain degree of attention and respect among the people of Hong Kong, particularly during the Lunar New Year period, although you couldn't really say that people had a lot of faith in it. Just as many people read their 'stars' in the daily newspapers, Chinese look forward to the predictions for the coming 12 months for their signs.

Historians do not know exactly how the astrological system developed out of the lunar calendar, which dates back to 2637BC and the Emperor Huang Ti. Legend says that the twelve animals signs were created at the time of the Lord Buddha, who one day commanded all beasts to report to him, but only twelve responded to the call. These were rewarded by having their names given to a specific year. The order in which they appeared, and their corresponding years, are as follows, along with the character traits each are supposed to include.

The Rat (1912, 1924, 1936, 1948, 1960, 1972, 1984, 1996)
The rat is charming and fun-loving, with a quick but controllable temper. Works hard for his money, but is generous to those he loves. Is inquisitive to the point of being downright nosy.

The Ox (1913, 1925, 1937, 1949, 1961, 1973, 1985, 1997)
The ox is a hard, plodding worker, logical, systematic and fair-minded, but tending to stubbornness. Very good when in authority or with responsibility.

The Tiger (1914, 1926, 1938, 1950, 1962, 1974, 1986, 1998)
The tiger commands respect from the other signs. It is fierce, warm-hearted, rebellious, obstinate, daring, passionate, sensitive and impulsive. Will go to the aid of others without thinking first.

The Rabbit (1915, 1927, 1939, 1951, 1963, 1975, 1987, 1999)
The rabbit symbolises longevity, refinement, kindness, and sensitivity to the arts. Tends to lead a reserved, tranquil life. Will avoid confrontations, although extremely cunning. Tends to mind his own business, and expects others to do likewise.

The Dragon (1916, 1928, 1940, 1952, 1964, 1976, 1988, 2000)
The dragon is known for his strength, honesty, decisiveness, energy, and ego. A benevolent creature, and perhaps the most propitious sign in the zodiac.

The Snake (1917, 1929, 1941, 1953, 1965, 1977, 1989, 2001)
The snake is the most intellectual and tenacious of all the signs. Enjoys the finer things in life and tends to be religious and psychic, although hedonistic and superstitious.

The Horse (1918, 1930, 1942, 1954, 1966, 1978, 1990, 2002)
The horse has great charm, wit and sexual appeal, although very sentimental and always falling in and out of love. Quick-tempered, self-indulgent, self-reliant, astute in money affairs, and unpredictable.

The Ram (1919, 1931, 1943, 1955, 1967, 1979, 1991, 2003)
The ram is the most gentle of the signs, and tends to be righteous, mild-mannered, artistic, creative and sometimes clairvoyant. Fussy and seldom happy with those around him, although well mannered and religious.

The Monkey (1920, 1932, 1944, 1956, 1968,. 1980, 1992, 2004)
The monkey is closest in character to man itself, therefore has intelligence, the ability to deceive, and is an opportunist. Also affable, clever, articulate, self-confidant, with a good sense of humour. These traits are balanced with selfishness, vanity, deceitfulness and jealousy.

The Rooster (1921, 1933, 1945, 1957, 1969, 1981, 1993, 2005)
The rooster likes to be noticed and speaks his opinion, irrespective of who is listening. Proud, though insecure & excellent with finances.

The Dog (1922, 1934, 1946, 1958, 1970, 1982, 1994, 2006)
The dog is a champion of justice, loyal, honest, intelligent, courageous and sexy, and a loner. Doesn't care much about money, but always seems to have it when he needs it.

The Pig (1923, 1935, 1947, 1959, 1971, 1983, 1995, 2007)
The pig also has high ideals, and no concern about money, but is stubborn and can take forever to make a decision. Not as flashy as some of the other signs, but is one of the most popular animals of the zodiac.

Festivals

Hong Kong follows ancient Chinese tradition when it comes to festivals, and hardly a month goes by when there is not at least one major cause for celebration. Some are so important that they rate a public holiday, others are more associated with families, or one particular religious belief. As the festivals are related to the phases of the moon, they are not on the same date each year. The Hong Kong Tourist Association offices have details of the actual dates.

Lunar New Year

This is the most important of all Chinese festivals and marks the beginning of the new lunar cycle. It is held between the winter solstice and the spring equinox (January/February) and is, in theory anyway, the beginning of spring. The holiday and the days that precede it are a time for cleaning the house, buying new clothes, settling debts, visiting relatives and friends, and exchanging gifts. Banks, some shops and other businesses close for at least three days, but usually longer.

Celebrations begin in the week leading up to the New Year, known as Little New Year.

The Festival has its origins in an old legend in which a wild beast (*nihn*, also the Cantonese word for 'year') devoured many villagers, at the end of each winter. The people discovered that the beast was frightened of bright lights, noise and the colour red, so to protect themselves, families made sure that on the 365th evening there were plenty of lights left on, anything possible was painted red, and that plenty of noise was generated with gongs, drums and crackers.

On the 24th day of the 12th moon, the Kitchen God leaves earth to report to the Jade Emperor in heaven on the behaviour of families during the past year. He is farewelled with offerings of wine, and people burn paper money and joss sticks, and to sweeten his words, special dumplings called *tang kwa* are smeared on his lips. The left-over dumplings are given to the children, and are a real delicacy.

The most festive day is the Lunar New Year Eve, when the entire family, living and dead, assemble for a reunion dinner, and are served symbolic food - abalone for abundance, pork and beans sprouts for prosperity, oysters for good business, fish for surplus. (This really seems to prove the first statement in the section on Religion.) After dinner, it is usual to visit one of the territory's flower markets, either the most famous at Victoria Peak on Hong Kong Island, or the smaller ones at Boundary Street, Shatin, Tai Po and Yuen Long. Flowers also have symbolic significance - peach and plum blossoms for good luck, chrysanthemum for happiness, and kumquat probably because the 'kum' is pronounced the same as the Chinese word for 'gold'.

Also on this day, strips of red paper with greetings of wealth, good fortune, longevity and the gift of sons, are pasted on doors, and new pictures of the Door Gods are put up. There are two legends concerning the origin of the Door Gods: one concerns two brothers who lived under a peach tree in a large orchard, and kept people safe by catching demons and throwing them to tigers; the other tells that a famous Tang Dynasty emperor who was protected from nightmares one night by the presence of two generals in his room, and so had portraits of them installed.

On the first day of the New Year, people visit temples to determine their future, and give packets of lucky money (*lai see*) to children and unmarried men and women. The present is accompanied by the words *"Kung Hei Fat Choy"*, which means "May you have a happy and prosperous New Year", and is said to bring good luck to the giver as well as the recipient. The packets are made of red and gold, and usually contain from HK$10 to HK$20.

The third day of the holiday is traditionally spent at home, and for a particularly human reason. It is thought that having spent the last two days together, tempers might be starting to fray and bickering could break out even in the best of families, and this is best done out of the public eye. It does have a special name though, being called "red-mouth quarrelling".

Yuen Siu (Spring Lantern) Festival

Yuen Siu marks the 15th and final day of the Lunar New Year holiday, and also the first full moon of the New Year. It dates back to the Han Dynasty (206BC-221AD) and celebrates the deposing of the hated Emperor Lu and his consort. It is also known as Chinese Valentine's Day, as on this day young, unmarried women would put on their best gear and head for the places where eligible men gathered. Although, of course, they were escorted, the festival often marked a temporary lifting of a government-imposed curfew.

The Chinese craft of lantern-making probably stems from this festival, and a master carpenter called Lu Pan. He lived during the Warring States Period, which means that the Chinese have been making fancy lanterns for about 2000 years. Lu Pan has his own festival in August.

During this festival you will see lanterns displayed in homes, shops, restaurants, temples and ancestral halls, although the main lantern festival is held in mid-Autumn.

Ching Ming Festival

This Confucian festival is held on the fourth or fifth day of the Third Moon (April) and is the first of two occasions that honour the dead each year. Dating back to the Han Dynasty (206BC-221AD), Ching Ming has people visiting ancestral graves and cleaning, repairing and painting them, offering meat, vegetables, wine and flowers, and burning gold and silver 'money' so the ancestors will have some pocket money in the afterworld. They also burn incense at the gravesides.

Ching Ming is a public holiday and a solemn occasion nowadays, but in ancient China it was also a celebration of the coming of spring and the day was spent playing sports including football, kite-flying and dog-racing.

Tin Hau Festival

Held on the twenty-third day of the Third Moon (April), this festival celebrates the birthday of Tin Hau, the Goddess of the Sea, and there are more than 24 temples in Hong Kong dedicated to her.

The legend of Tin Hau dates from the early 12th century, when a young girl saved her two brothers from drowning during a terrible storm. Fisherfolk pray to her for calm waters, large catches, protection from shipwrecks and sickness, today.

Festivities include colourful parades, Chinese opera performances, and the sailing of hundreds of decorated junks and sampans through the waterways to the Tin Hau temples.

Tam Kung Festival

Tam Kung is also a popular deity with fisherfolk, and residents of Shau Kei Wan on Hong Kong Island believe him responsible for saving many lives during a cholera outbreak in 1967. He is a Taoist child-god whose powers developed when he was twelve years old. He could heal the sick, predict the future, and control the weather.

Celebrations are held at the Tam Kung Temple in Shau Kei Wan on the eighth day of the Fourth Moon (May). The temple is at the end of Shau Kei Wan Main Street East, near the waterfront, and to see the procession it is best to get there before midday.

Birthday of Lord Buddha

Also held on the eighth day of the Fourth Moon, this festival commemorates the birth, in the 6th century, of Prince Siddhartha Sakyamuni, the founder of Buddhism.

The birthday is observed in all Buddhist temples in Hong Kong, but there is a special celebration at the 10,000 Buddhas Monastery in Shatin - the Buddha-Bathing Ceremony. This sees the washing of the image of Buddha with spice-scented water, symbolising the washing away of sins.

Cheung Chau Bun Festival

Although this festival is usually held in late April/early May, its exact date is chosen by divination, and the Tourist Association has the details.

The festival is only celebrated in Hong Kong, and stems from the belief that restless and hungry ghosts roam the usually peaceful island of Cheung Chau at this time. The ghosts are supposedly of hundreds of islanders who were massacred by pirates a century ago, or they are of the animals and fish that were killed and consumed throughout the year. In any case, the Bun Festival is held to placate them, and during the week no meat or fish is eaten on the island, and paper houses, cars and money are burnt.

Symbols of the festival are three 20m conical towers built of bamboo and paper and covered with sweet pink and white buns, and until recently, at the end of the festival young men would scramble up to the top of the towers to get a bun from the top, which was supposed to bring very good luck. Now the buns are distributed by hand, which is much safer, although less spectacular.

One feature that has remained is the 'floating' children. Kids between the ages of five and eight are supported by a system of hidden rods and wires and seem to float among the crowds in a procession. They are heavily made up and dressed to represent figures in Chinese history and mythology.

There are also lion, unicorn and dragon dances, Chinese opera performances, traditional rites at the Pak Tai Temple, and a carnival atmosphere all over the island.

Tuen Ng (Dragon Boat) Festival

A major festival, held on the fifth day of the Fifth Moon (May), commemorates the death of a national hero, Ch'u Yuen, in the 3rd century BC. He drowned himself in protest against a corrupt government, and the villages who witnessed the event tried to save his life by beating the water with their paddles to scare off demons, and throwing dumplings into the sea to feed the fish so they wouldn't eat Ch'u Yuen.

Today, narrow boats decorated with the head and tail of a dragon race each other, with the accompaniment of much drum beating and noise, and special dumplings are made, which are offered for sale. Races are held at many locations - Hong Kong Island, Kowloon and the New Territories, including Stanley, Aberdeen, Shau Kei Wan, Chai Wan, Yau Ma Tei, Shatin, Tai Po, Sai Kung, Tuen Mun, and on the outlying islands.

Dragon Boat Festival International Races

The tradition of dragon boat racing has caught on around the world, and a week before or after the local festival is held, the International Races see teams from many overseas countries. For these races, the boats are built to strict specifications, and the crew must not exceed 22 people, of whom one must be the drummer and one a steersman.

Held in early June along the Tsimshatsui East waterfront in Kowloon, special tours are available to view the races from boats moored in the harbour. Contact the Hong Kong Tourist Association for details.

Birthday of Lu Pan

Lu Pan was born on the thirteenth day of the Sixth Moon (August) in 507BC, and was an architect, engineer and inventor. He is the Taoist patron of carpenters and builders, and is credited with inventing the drill, the plane, the shovel, the saw, the lock and the ladder. He apparently had a lot in

common with his wife, who invented, amongst other things, the umbrella.

On Lu Pan's birthday, people connected with the construction industry hold banquets to celebrate and thank the god for good fortune during the past year, and to pray for an even better next year. There is only one temple in Hong Kong dedicated to Lu Pan, in Sands Street, Kennedy Town, and on his birthday people gather here to pay their respects at noon.

Seven Sisters Festival

Also called the Maiden's Festival, it is celebrated on the seventh day of the Seventh Moon (August) in China and Hong Kong. The festival comes from an ancient Chinese legend in which an orphaned cowherd is thrown out of home by his elder brother and sister-in-law, with only an ox, a broken-down cart, and a tiny piece of land.

The sympathetic ox (called Elder Brother the Ox) tells the young man that on a certain day seven girls will come to earth to take a bath in a nearby river. If the young man steals the clothes of one of the girls, she will marry him. Well he did, and she did, and they lived happily for three years, until the girl was ordered back to heaven, only to see her husband on one day of the year. The husband eventually died, and of course, became immortal, but the Queen Mother of the Western Heaven, who was obviously a spoil-sport, drew a line across the sky to keep the two apart, and they could still only see each other on the special day. The line she drew, by the way, was the Milky Way.

The festival is observed in two ways - on the sixth day, unmarried men pay homage to the cowherd; and on the seventh day, young unmarried women make offerings to the Seventh Maiden.

The celebrations mainly take place in the home, but young women looking for a husband have been known to visit Lover's Rock, in Bowen Road on Hong Kong Island, where joss sticks are burned and soothsayers ply their trade.

Yue Lan (Hungry Ghosts) Festival

The fifteenth day of the Seventh Moon (September) is the time when the gates of the underworld are opened and angry, hungry ghosts are free to wander around. Offerings, in the shape of paper replicas of material possessions and money, are made to try to placate them, and all is watched over by the towering paper figure of Prince Daih Su. When he is satisfied with the gifts offered, he returns to heaven in a burst of flames, presumably taking the ghosts with him.

Apparently the exact day of the ghosts appearance is not entirely trusted, and for weeks before and after the festival it is common to see people burning paper offerings outside their shops and homes.

Mid-Autumn Festival

Held on the fifteenth day of the Eighth Moon, when the moon is said to be at its fullest and brightest, the Mid-Autumn Festival celebrates the year's harvest. Of course, there are many legends connected with the holiday, including that which gives birth to its most popular symbol, the moon cake. During China's 14th century revolt against the Mongols, Chu Yuan Chang and his deputy plotted to overthrow a strategic walled city held by the enemy. The deputy, dressed as a Taoist priest, entered the city and gave out moon cakes containing the message "revolt on the night of the full moon". The revolt succeeded and formed the basis of the Ming Dynasty. Moon cakes today are filled with sesame or lotus-seed paste, red bean paste and even meat and duck's egg yolks.

The festival's other symbol is the lantern, and on the day of the festival crowds of people make their way through the streets to the public parks armed with lanterns, often in the shape of symbolic animals and birds.

Birthday of Confucius

Although not widely celebrated in Hong Kong, the birthday of the man who may have had the most influence on China's history is observed by many. Confucius was born in 551BC, during the Warring States Period, and developed a system of ethics and politics which stressed self-enlightenment through the Five Virtues - charity, justice, propriety, wisdom and loyalty. His birthday is on the twenty-seventh day of the Eighth Moon (October).

Chung Yeung Festival

This is a Confucian holiday, celebrated on the ninth day of the Ninth Moon (October), and is the second family remembrance day of the year. The people head for the graves of their ancestors, make offerings, tend to the graves, then eat the offerings at the graveside.

The legend attached to this day also has people setting off for high places. During the Han Dynasty, scholar Woon King was warned of impending disaster, so he took his family to the top of a hill near their home. When they returned, they found that their cattle and poultry were all dead, so they gave thanks that they had been spared.

On this day the cemeteries are full of people, and there's not much spare room on any of the hills either, especially the Peak.

Entry Regulations

All visitors must have a valid passport. Citizens of some 24 countries, including the USA and certain Western European and South American nations, are permitted one-month visa-free visits. Three-month visa-free visits are available to another 23 countries, which include Britain's dependent territories and all the Commonwealth countries. The British themselves can obtain a six-month visa-free stay.

Visitors are allowed to bring into the territory duty free - a one-litre bottle of alcohol together with 200 cigarettes (or 50 cigars or 250g of tobacco); 60 millilitres of perfume and 250 millilitres of toilet water are also permitted.

Firearms must be declared and handed over for safe-keeping until departure.

The import and export of raw or worked ivory has strict regulations. Visitors who purchase any ivory products in Hong Kong (regardless of the amount) have to obtain an import licence from their country of residence, as well as an export licence to take the ivory out of Hong Kong. The Government of Hong Kong is a contracting party to CITES (Convention on International Trade in Endangered Species) and as such is committed to the protection of the African elephant. Anyone who breaches the regulations on licences is liable to prosecution, resulting in a fine and forfeiture of the ivory.

An International Certificate of Vaccination against Cholera is only necessary if you have been in an infected area during the 14 days prior to your arrival. However, health requirements can change suddenly, so check with your travel agent, especially if you are travelling on to other parts of Asia.

Exit Regulations

There is an airport departure tax of HK$100 for everyone 12 years and over. For travel to Macau there is a departure tax of HK$26, which is usually included in the fare.

Diplomatic Missions

Australia: Australian Consulate General, 23-24F Harbour Centre, 25 Harbour Road, Wanchai, ph 2827 8881, open Mon-Fri 9am-noon, 2-4pm.

Canada: The Commission for Canada, 12/F Tower 1 Exchange Square, 8 Connaught Place, Central, ph 2810 4321, open Mon-Fri 8am-noon, Mon-Tues, Thurs-Fri 1.30-4.30pm.

New Zealand: NZ High Commission, 3414 Jardine House, Connaught Place, ph 2525 5044, 2877 4488 (Visa Section), open Mon-Fri 8.30am-1pm, 2-5pm.

Singapore: Unit 901-2, 9F, Tower 1 Admiralty Centre, 18 Harcourt Road, Wanchai, ph 2527 2212/4, open Mon-Fri 10am-12.30pm, 2.30-5.30pm.

United States: American Consulate, 26 Garden Road, Central District, ph 2523 9011, open Mon-Fri 8.30am-12.30pm, 1.30-5.30pm.

United Kingdom: Immigration Department, Wanchai Tower 2, 7 Gloucester Road, Wanchai, ph 2824 6111, open Mon-Fri 8.45am-4.30pm, Sat 9-11.30am.

Money

The unit of currency is the Hong Kong dollar (HK$). Notes are issued by the HongkongBank and the Standard Chartered Bank in denominations of $1000, $500, $100, $50, $20 and $10.

Silver coins are for $5, $2 and $1, and there are bronze coins for 50c, 20c and 10c.

Approximate exchange rates, which should be used as a guide only, are as follows:

A$1 =	HK$4.70
NZ$1 =	HK$4.00
US$1 =	HK$7.70
UK£ =	- HK$12.80
CAN$1 =	HK$5.20

There are no restrictions on currencies being brought in or taken out of Hong Kong.

Currency is easily changed either at banks, hotels, or money-changers. Check the exchange rates before handing over your money or travellers cheques.

American Express cardholders now have access to Jetco automated teller machines, and can withdraw local currency and travellers cheques at the Express Cash ATM at New World Tower, Central.

Holders of Visa card, Mastercard and other cards authorised by HongkongBank can also obtain local currency from HongkongBank 'Electronic Money' ATMs at the airport and other convenient locations.

There is also EA$YXCHANGE which is a 24 hour automated currency exchange. Locations are in the Wing Lung Bank, 4 Carnarvon Road, Tsim Sha Tsui, Kowloon, and Shop101 Convention Plaza, Wan Chai, Hong Kong Island.

Communications

Post Offices

The main post office on Hong Kong Island is in Central, behind Jardine House, next to the Star Ferry (open Mon-Fri 8am-6pm, Sat 8am-2pm). In Kowloon, it is at 405 Nathan Road, between Jordan and Yau Ma Tei MTR stations (open Mon-Fri 9.30am-6pm, Sat 9.30am-1pm).

Post offices are closed on Sundays and public holidays.

For further enquiries, ph 2523 1071/2 or 2780 8598 from 9am-5pm.

Telephones

Free for local calls from private phones, though some hotels have a handling charge. Public phone booths cost HK$1. Emergency calls are free on 999.
For Directory Enquiries, call 108.

Long-distance calls can be made from International Direct Dialling Public Coin Phones, from HK Telecom International Ltd offices, and by Cardphone.

International calls on a collect-call basis are available on the push-button call-home system, which gives immediate connection with the operator of the country required. This service is available throughout Hong Kong. Dial 013 for information on dial access numbers and details on phone locations, purchase and operation of stored value cards and Coin Phone. Stored value cards can also be bought at HKTA Information and Gift Centres.

The IDD code for Hong Kong is 852.

Newspapers

There are four English language newspapers printed in Hong Kong: the *South China Morning Post*, (HK$4); *The Hong Kong Standard*, (HK$4); *The Asian Wall Street Journal*, (HK$7); and the *International Herald Tribune*, (HK$7).

Television

Two English language channels broadcast from mid-afternoon to late evening with a selection of locally produced items, plus features from Britain, America and Australia. Also Star TV and Cable TV are now available.

Radio

The main English language radio stations are Radio 3, broadcast on 567 kHz, Radio 4 (classical music) on 97.6 and 98.9 mHz, and Commercial Radio on 864kHz. The BBC World Service, broadcast from London, is relayed from 4am-12.15am on 675 kHz.

Miscellaneous

Weights and Measures

Hong Kong is gradually going metric. Taxis run on kilometres, whereas heights/lengths are still given in both measures.

Metrification is not aided by the fact that the Chinese have their own system of weights and measures. Market produce, for example, is sold by the catty, which is 1.3 lbs or 600g. Gold is sold by the tael, which is 1.3 ounces or 38g.

Electricity is simpler. The voltage is 200/220 volts, 50 cycles. Most hotels have shaver adapters.

Banks
Banks are open Mon-Fri and usually Saturday morning, however there are differences in the actual hours from branch to branch. Both The HongkongBank and Standard Chartered Bank are open Mon-Fri 9am-4.30pm, Sat 9am-12.30pm, while the Hang Seng Bank is open Mon-Fri 9am-5pm, Sat 9am-1pm. Also, some banking transactions finish about an hour before closing time.

Business Hours
Most offices are open Mon-Fri 9am-5pm, (closed for lunch 1-2pm) and Sat 9am-1pm.

Shops are open seven days, although some department stores close on Sunday. In the Central District hours are 10am-6pm; Causeway Bay and Wanchai, 10am-9.30pm; Tsimshatsui, 10am-9 or 10pm; East Tsimshatsui, 10am-7.30pm.

Water
All water direct from government mains in Hong Kong complies with the United Nations World Health Organisation standards, and is fit for drinking. The water supply in some parts of the New Territories and Outlying Islands is from wells, and is less reliable. Bottled water is widely available in hotels and supermarkets.

Tipping
Most restaurants add 10% automatically, but it is expected that loose change will be left for the staff. Where tipping is left up to you, 10% is considered acceptable.

Just remember that everyone who does something for you expects something in return.

Police

If you wish to ask directions, or get help of any kind, keep in mind that policemen who speak English wear a red flash under their shoulder number.

Identification

All residents of Hong Kong are required to carry an identity card at all times. It is a good idea also for visitors to carry some form of identification with a photograph, such as a drivers licence or, of course, your passport.

Disabled Visitors

The Hong Kong Tourist Association puts out a handy free booklet entitled *A Guide for Physically Handicapped Visitors to Hong Kong*, and it lists more than 200 places, including hotels, restaurants, shops, and sightseeing venues.

Emergency Telephone Numbers

Police, Fire, Ambulance - 999.
Police, Crime Hotline (also taxi complaints) - 2527 7177.
General enquiries - 2860 3903.
Free Ambulance Service - Hong Kong Island - 2576 6555.
Kowloon - 2713 5555.
Queen Mary Hospital, Pokfulam Road, HK, ph 2819 2111.
Hong Kong Adventist Hospital, 40 Stubbs Road, HK,
ph 2574 6211.
Queen Elizabeth Hospital, Wylie Road, Kowloon, ph 2710 2111.
**There are no 24-hour chemists (drugstores) in Hong Kong.
For urgent medication contact one of the above hospitals.**

Time Zone

Standard time is Greenwich Mean Time, plus 8 hours. Hong Kong does not have daylight saving.

When it is noon in Hong Kong, the time in the following places is:

Eastern Australia - 2pm
Western Australia - noon
New Zealand - 4pm
London - 4am
USA (West) - 8pm, the previous day
USA (East) - 11pm, the previous day.

Travel Information

How to Get There

By Air
Ansett Australia have flights to Hong Kong from Sydney daily except Mon, Thurs.

Cathay Pacific is Hong Kong's flag carrier and they have flights to Hong Kong from:
  Auckland - daily
  Bangkok - daily
  Brisbane - Wed, Thurs, Sat, Sun
  London - daily
  Los Angeles - daily
  Melbourne - daily
  Singapore - daily
  Sydney - daily
  Vancouver - daily

British Airways have flights to Hong Kong from:
  Birmingham - daily
  Edinburgh - daily
  Glasgow - daily
  London - daily
  Manchester - daily
  Newcastle - daily.

Qantas has flights from:
  Adelaide - daily
  Brisbane - daily
  Canberra - daily via Sydney
  Hobart - daily via Sydney, except Tues, Wed via Melbourne
  Melbourne - daily
  Perth - daily
  Sydney - daily.

Sampans at sunset

Peach blossoms in the flower market at Lunar New Year.

A child seems to walk on air at the Cheung Chau Bun Festival

Air New Zealand has flights from:
  Auckland - Tues, Thurs and Sun
  Christchurch - Tues, Thurs and Sun via Auckland
  Wellington - Tues, Thurs and Sun via Auckland.

United Airlines
  Los Angeles - daily
  San Francisco - daily
  Honolulu - daily

Canadian Airlines has flights from:
  Montreal - daily
  Toronto - daily
  Vancouver - daily

Thai Airlines have daily flights from Bangkok to Hong Kong.

Singapore Airlines have daily flights Singapore to Hong Kong.

Hong Kong has a new airport facility which cost some US$20 billion at Check Lap Kok (CLK). It is four times the size of the previous Kai Tak Airport which is now closed. The new airport is the largest covered structure in the world. An internal shuttle train runs beween east and west halls and there are plenty of moving walkways to move around the 1.2 kilometre long terminal. There are some 140+ shops plus 25 food and beverage outlets.

The Passenger terminal building is airconditioned. It houses SkyMart, banks, a post office, police report centre, pay phones, help phones, money exchange outlets, nursing rooms, a business centre, hotel reservation centres, left-luggage service, prayer rooms, VIP lounges. The Hong Kong Tourist Association has information centres in the Halls A&B on the arrival level. Also, free phone calls are available in the Arrivals Hall and in the baggage claim area. Information flight and general information available on 2181-8888.

Rail
From the Airport:
The airport has been built on the island of Chek Lap Kok and is

connected to Lantau Island by a massive bridge, with another 2.2 kilometres long linking this island with Tsing Yi. A high speed railway (AEL) has been built linking the airport with Kowloon Station (HK$90 [US$11.50] one way), Hong Kong Station in Central (HK$100 [US$13] one way). Trains operate from 6am to 1am daily at 8 minute intervals.

To the Airport:
Free airport express shuttle services are provided to AEL passengers. There are 4 circular routes running between 17 hotels and the Hong Kong and Kowloon AEL stations. Services are provided daily between 6am and 1am at 15 minutes intervals. Passengers departing overseas can also check-in at either Kowloon or Hong Kong Stations. I must admit I would prefer to do it at the airport, but ask advice from the Concierge at your Hotel.

Buses
There are 6 airbuses dedicated to departing and arriving passengers. They have fewer stops than the conventional lines and stop at all major hotels. They are air conditioned and have luggage racks. Tickets can be obtained at the Customer Service counter in the Arrivals Hall.

Taxis
All Hong Kong taxis are licensed, air-conditioned and metered. Red Taxis serve Hong Kong Island and Kowloon. Green taxis serve the New Territories, and blue taxis serve Lantau Island.

Estimates of costs are the following:
Airport to Hong Kong Island
to Central	HK$350.00 (39km)
Airport to Causeway Bay	HK$335.00 (40km)

Airport to Kowloon
to Tsim Sha Tsui	HK$285 (36km)
to Kwun Tong	HK$320 (41km)

Airport to New Territories
Tsuen Wan	HK$230 (28km)
Sha Tin	HK$325 (41km)

By Sea
Several companies have luxury cruise liners calling into Hong Kong, and your travel agent is the best to ask for advice on these.

By Rail
The only time visitors arrive by train is if they have been travelling in China. The Kowloon-Canton Railway (KCR) runs between Lo Wu on the Chinese border to Hung Hom in Kowloon, and for information on timetables and fares, ph 2807 6177. Actually, it is possible to travel from London by train, through Europe, the Russia and China!

Package Tours
Many people travelling to Hong Kong do so independently, thinking that package tours are more applicable to travelling to several destinations on one holiday, whereas Hong Kong is often a one-stop trip. Nevertheless there are many packages available to Hong Kong, often advertised as 'shopping getaways'. They offer the usual reduced rates for accommodation and air fares, and provide transfers to and from the airport, and some throw in vouchers for discount shopping. The packages are generally around 5-6 nights, with extra nights available at discounted rates. Optional excursions are available to local attractions, and to China and Macau, also at reduced rates.

Tourist Information
Hong Kong Tourist Association information and gift centres are found at the airport (for arriving passengers), and at:

Star Ferry Concourse, Kowloon - open Mon-Fri 8am-6pm, Sat-Sun and public holidays 9am-5pm.

Shop 8, Basement, Jardine House, 1 Connaught Place, Central - open Mon-Fri 9am-6pm, Sat 9am-1pm.

The Association also has a multilingual telephone information service on 2807 6177, Mon-Fri 8am-6pm, Sat-Sun and public holidays 9am-5pm.

The logo of the Hong Kong Tourist Association is a red sampan in a red circle, and it is advisable to shop and eat where this sign is displayed. It does not mean that the Tourist

Association is responsible for the actions of the particular establishment, but it will investigate any complaints with regard to service, value for money, accurate representation of products or the establishment's reaction to initial complaints.

The Association will also give shopping advice, or you can make enquiries about their members by phoning 2807 6177, Mon-Fri 9am-5pm, Sat 9am-12.45pm.

The HKTA publish several booklets and brochures that tell everything you need to know to get the most out of your stay in Hong Kong.

Accommodation

The Hong Kong Tourist Association brochures say there are 33,500 rooms to let in the Territory, and that is no exaggeration. All the major international hotel chains are represented, often with more than one establishment, and the local and regional groups vie with them for opulence and service. There are also smaller hotels, with a more family style atmosphere, guest houses and hostels. Normally around mid year May to August you can get reasonable deals of up to 40% off the rack rate. Most hotels have a hotel doctor.

Here is a selection, with **prices in Hong Kong dollars** for a double room per night, which should be used as a guide only.

All accommodation prices are subject to a 13% service charge/government tax.

Hotels

Hong Kong Island

Luxury
Grand Hyatt Hong Kong, 1 Harbour Road, Wanchai, ph 2588 1234, www.hyatt.com - 572 rooms, restaurant (American, Cantonese, English, Italian, Japanese), bar and lounge, coffee shop, swimming pool, health centre, disco/nightclub, tour desk - HK$3150-$3,950.

Mandarin Oriental, 5 Connaught Road, Central, ph 2522 0111 - 541 rooms, restaurants (Cantonese, French, Grill), bar and lounge, coffee shop, health centre, swimming pool, disco/nightclub, tour desk - HK$3,000.

Conrad International Hotel, Pacific Place, 88 Queensway, ph 2521 3838, www.hilton.com - 513 rooms, restaurants (Asian, Chinese, Italian, Western), bar and lounge, coffee shop, health centre, swimming pool, tour desk - $3,050 - $4,150.

J.W. Marriott Hong Kong, Pacific Place, 88 Queensway, Central, ph 2810 8366, www.marriott.com/hongkong/ 210head text.html - 604 rooms, restaurants (American, Cantonese), bar and lounge, coffee shop, health centre, swimming pool, tour desk - $2650-3800.

First Class

New World Harbour View, 1 Harbour Road, Wanchai, ph 2802 8888 - 862 rooms, restaurants (Cantonese, European, International), bar and lounge, coffee shop, health centre, pool, disco/nightclub, tour desk - $2730-3530.

Hotel Furama, 1 Connaught Road, Central, ph 2525 5111, www.hkta.org/adverts/furama.html - 523 rooms, restaurants (Cantonese, Continental, International buffet, Japanese), bar and lounge, coffee shop, health centre, tour desk - $2350-3,300.

Standard

The Park Lane, 310 Gloucester Road, Causeway Bay, ph 2890 3355 - 850 rooms, restaurants (Continental, Asian), bar and lounge, coffee shop, health centre, disco/nightclub, tour desk - $2480-3,680.

The Excelsior Hotel, 281 Gloucester Road, Causeway Bay, ph 2895 8888, www.empire-hotel.com - 913 rooms, restaurants (Chinese, Continental, Italian, Euro-asian), bar and lounge, coffee shop, tour desk - $2500-3400.

Regal Hongkong Hotel, 88 yee Wo Street, Causeway Bay, ph 2890 6633 - 425 rooms, restaurants (Cantonese, Chiu Chow, International, Mediterranean), bar and lounge, swimming pool, health centre, coffee shop, tour desk - $2,800-3,800.

Luk Kwok Hotel, 72 Gloucester Road, Wanchai, ph 2866 2166, www.lukkwokhotel.com - 198 rooms, restaurants (Cantonese, Continental), tour desk - $1,800-2,600.

City Garden Hotel, 9 City Garden Road, North Point, ph 2887 2888 - 617 rooms, restaurants (International, Cantonese), bar and lounge, coffee shop, swimming pool, tour desk - $1,700-2,300.

Grand Plaza Hotel, 2 Kornhill Road, Quarry Bay, ph 2886 0011

- 248 rooms, restaurant (Cantonese), bar and lounge, coffee shop, health centre, indoor swimming pool, tour desk - $1,350-2,400.

Century Hong Kong Hotel, 238 Jaffe Road, Wanchai, ph 2598 8888 - 516 rooms, restaurants (Italian), bar and lounge, coffee shop, swimming pool, health centre, tour desk - $1,900-2,550.

Budget

The Wesley, 22 Hennessy Road, Wanchai, ph 2866 6688 - 251 rooms, restaurant (International), bar and lounge, coffee shop, tour desk - $1,300-2,550.

New Harbour Hotel, 41-49 Hennessy Road, Wanchai, ph 2861 1166 - 173 rooms, business centre, coffee shop, tour desk - $1,080-1,680.

Harbour View International House, 4 Harbour Road, Wanchai, ph 2802 0111 - 320 rooms, restaurant (American), lounge and bar, coffee shop, tour desk - $1,050-1,550.

New Cathay Hotel, 17 Tung Lo Wan Road, Causeway Bay, ph 2577 8211 - 223 rooms, restaurant (Cantonese), coffee shop, tour desk - $980-1,300.

Kowloon/New Territories

Luxury

The Peninsula, Salisbury Road, Tsimshatsui, ph 2366 6251, www.peninsula.com/phk.htm - 156 rooms, restaurants (Cantonese, Continental, French, International, Swiss), bar and lounge, coffee shop, tour desk - $2,700-4,300.

Kowloon Shangri-La Hotel, 64 Mody Road, Tsimshatsui East, ph 2721 2111, www.shangri-la.com - 719 rooms, restaurants (Cantonese, French Mediterranean, Californian, Continental, Japanese), bar and lounge, coffee shop, health centre, swimming pool, disco/nightclub - $2,700-4,050.

First Class

Hotel Nikko Hong Kong, 72 Mody Road, Tsimshatsui East, ph 2739 1111, www.hotelnikko.com.hk - 461 rooms, restaurants (Cantonese, French, Japanese), bar and lounge, health centre, swimming pool, tour desk - $5,500-13,500.

The Regent, Salisbury Road, Tsimshatsui, ph 2721 1211 - 602 rooms, restaurants (American, Cantonese, European), bar and lounge, coffee shop, health centre, swimming pool, tour desk - $2,500-4,150.

Hong Kong Renaissance Hotel, 8 Peking Road, Tsimshatsui, ph 2375 1133 - 495 rooms, restaurants (American, Cantonese, International), bar and lounge, coffee shop, health centre, swimming pool - $2,350-3,150.

Hyatt Regency, 67 Nathan Road, Tsimshatsui, ph 2311 1234 - 723 rooms, restaurants (Cantonese, Continental, Japanese), bar and lounge, coffee shop, tour desk, disabled rooms - $2,500-3,800.

New World Hotel, 22 Salisbury Road, Tsimshatsui, ph 2369 4111 - 543 rooms, restaurant (European, Cantonese), bar and lounge, coffee shop, health centre, swimming pool, disco/nightclub, tour desk - $2,250-2,600.

Sheraton Hong Kong Hotel & Towers, 20 Nathan Road, Tsimshatsui, ph 369 1111, www.sheraton.com/quickview/ h0482.html - 804 rooms, restaurants (American, Cantonese, Continental, Indian, Japanese), bar and lounge, coffee shop, health centre, swimming pool, tour desk - $2,500-3,680.

Grand Stanford Harbour View, 70 Mody Road, Tsimshatsui East, ph 2721 5161 - 597 rooms, restaurants (Cantonese, French, Italian, International), bar and lounge, coffee shop, health centre, swimming pool, tour desk - $2,350-3,750.

The Hongkong Hotel, Harbour City, 3 Canton Road, Tsimshatsui, ph 2113 0088 - 709 rooms, restaurants (Cantonese, Chiu Chow, Continental, Japanese, American, International), bar and lounge, coffee shop, swimming pool, tour desk - $2,300-4,050.

The Royal Garden Hotel, 69 Mody Road, Tsimshatsui East, ph 2721 5215, www.theroyalgardenhotel.com.hk - 420 rooms, restaurants (Cantonese, European, Italian, Japanese), bar and lounge, coffee shop, disco/nightclub, tour desk - $2,250-2,750.

Regal Kowloon, 71 Mody Road, Tsimshatsui East, ph 2722 1818, www.regal-hotels.com - 591 rooms, restaurants (American, Cantonese, French, Japanese), bar and lounge, coffee shop, health centre, disco/nightclub, tour desk - $2,200-3,050.

Marco Polo Hotel, Harbour City, Canton Road, Tsimshatsui, ph 2113 0088 - 440 rooms, restaurants (Continental, French, Tea Room), bar and lounge, coffee shop, tour desk - $1200-1350.

The Prince Hotel, Harbour City, Canton Road, Tsimshatsui,

ph 2113 1888 - restaurant (International, South-east Asian), bar and lounge, coffee shop, swimming pool, tour desk - $1,950-2,450.

Standard

The Royal Pacific Hotel & Towers, China Hong Kong City, 33 Canton Road, Tsimshatsui, www.royalpacific.com.hk, ph 236 1188 - 649 rooms, restaurant (Swiss), bar and lounge, coffee shop, health centre, tour desk - $1,850-3,450.

Holiday Inn Golden Mile, 46-52 Nathan Road, Tsimshatsui, ph 2369 3111, www.goldenmile.com - 594 rooms, restaurants (American, Cantonese, German), bar and lounge, coffee shop, health centre, swimming pool, tour desk - $2,300-2,550.

Miramar Hotel, 130 Nathan Road, Tsimshatsui, ph 2368 1111, www.great-china.net/hotelmiramar - 526 rooms, restaurants (Cantonese), bar and lounge, coffee shop, tour desk - $1,400-2,800.

Park Hotel, 61-65 Chatham Road South, Tsimshatsui, ph 2366 1371, www.hkta.org/adverts/parkfact.html - 430 rooms, restaurants (American, Cantonese), bar and lounge, coffee shop, tour desk - $1,800-1,900.

Windsor Hotel, 39-43A Kimberley Road, Tsimshatsui, ph 2739 5665 - 166 rooms, restaurant (Cantonese), bar and lounge, coffee shop, tour desk - $1,400-1,800.

Eaton Hotel, 380 Nathan Road, Yaumati, ph 2782 1818 - 468 rooms, restaurants (Asian, Cantonese, Western), bar and lounge, coffee shop - $1,300-2,180.

Regal Riverside, Tai Chung Kiu Road, Shatin, ph 2649 7878, www.regal-hotels.com/riverside.html - 833 rooms, restaurants (Cantonese, International, Thai, Western), bar and lounge, coffee shop, health centre, swimming pool, disco/nightclub, tour desk - $2,000-2,400.

Royal Park Hotel, 8 Pak Hok Ting Street, Shatin, ph 2601 2111 - 442 rooms, restaurants (Chiu Chow, Japanese, Western, Eastern), bar and lounge, coffee shop, health centre, indoor swimming pool, tour desk - $1,780-2,480.

Kowloon Hotel, 19-21 Nathan Road, Tsimshatsui, ph 2369 8698 - 707 rooms, restaurants (Cantonese, Italian), bar and lounge, coffee shop, tour desk - $1,380-2,500.

The Kimberley Hotel, 28 Kimberley Road, Tsimshatsui, ph 2723 2888, www.kimberley.com.hk - 546 rooms, restaurants

(Cantonese, Japanese, International), bar and lounge, coffee shop, health centre, tour desk - $1,500-1,950.

Majestic Hotel, 348 Nathan Road, Yau Ma Tei, ph 2781 1333 - 387 rooms, restaurant, bar and lounge, coffee shop, 'disabled' facilities, tour desk - $1,450-1900.

Grand Tower Hotel, 627-641 Nathan Road, Mong Kok, ph 2789 0011 - 549 rooms, restaurants (International, Chinese), bar and lounge, coffee shop, tour desk - $1,400-2,050.

New Astor Hotel, 11 Carnarvon Road, Tsimshatsui, ph 2366 7261 - 151 rooms, restaurants (Cantonese, Western), coffee shop, tour desk - $1,200-1,700.

The Metropole Hotel, 75 Waterloo Road, Kowloon, ph 2761 1711, www.metropole.com.hk - 487 rooms, restaurants (Cantonese, International), bar and lounge, coffee shop, swimming pool, tour desk - $1,330-1,980.

Regal Airport Hotel, Sa Po Road, Kowloon City, ph 2718 0333 - 385 rooms, restaurants (British, Cantonese, Chiu Chow, French), bar and lounge, coffee shop - $1,850-2,700.

Guangdong Hotel, 18 Prat Avenue, Tsimshatsui, ph 2739 3311, www.gdihml.com.hk - 245 rooms, restaurants (American, Cantonese, European), coffee shop, tour desk - $1,380-1,780.

Budget
Nathan Hotel, 378 Nathan Road, Yau Ma Tei, ph 2388 5141 - 186 rooms, restaurant (Cantonese, American), coffee shop, tour desk - $1,200-1,350.

Concourse Hotel, 20-46 Lai Chi Kok Road, Mong Kok, ph 2397 6683, www.hkstar.com/concourse - 359 rooms, restaurants (Cantonese, Korean, Continental), bar and lounge, coffee shop, tour desk - $1,180-2,080.

Imperial, 30-34 Nathan Road, Tsimshatsui, ph 2366 2201, www.imperialhotel.com.hk - 214 rooms, bar & restaurant (Cantonese, Italian), tour desk - $1,100-2,000.

International Hotel, 33 Cameron Road, Tsimshatsui, ph 2366 3381 - 89 rooms, restaurants (International), bar and lounge, coffee shop, tour desk - $780-1,080.

Bangkok Royal Hotel, 2-12 Pilkem Street, Yau Ma Tei, ph 2735 9181 - 70 rooms, restaurants (American, Thai, Cantonese), bar and lounge, coffee shop, tour desk - $580-740.

Shamrock Hotel, 223 Nathan Road, Yau Ma Tei, ph 2735 2271 - 148 rooms, restaurants (American, Malaysian), bar and lounge, coffee shop, tour desk - $950-1,170.

King's Hotel, 473-473A Nathan Road, Yau Ma Tei, ph 2780 1281 - 72 rooms, restaurants (American, Thai, Cantonese), coffee shop - $670-700.

Outlying Islands
Cheung Chau Warwick Hotel, East Bay, Cheung Chau Island, ph 2981 0081 - 70 rooms, restaurants (European, Cantonese), bar and lounge, coffee shop, swimming pool, - $620-1,080.

Hostels and Guest Houses
'The Salisbury', YMCA of Hong Kong, 41 Salisbury Road, Tsimshatsui, ph 2369 2211 - 398 rooms, restaurants (American, Asian, Continental), coffee shop, indoor swimming pool tour desk - $1,030-2000.

Garden View International House (YWCA), 1 MacDonnell Road, Central, ph 2877 3737 - 131 rooms, coffee shop, swimming pool, tour desk - $880-990.

YMCA International House, 23 Waterloo Road, Yau Ma Tei, ph 2771 9111 - 277 rooms, restaurant (American), health centre, tour desk - $880-1,100.

Caritas Bianchi Lodge, 4 Cliff Road, Yau Ma Tei, ph 2388 1111 - 90 rooms, restaurants (Cantonese, International), coffee shop, tour desk - $820-1,200.

Ann Black Guest House (YMCA), 5 Man Fuk Road, Waterloo Hill Road, Kowloon, ph 2713 9211 - 171 rooms, restaurant (American, Cantonese), coffee shop - $510-780.

Booth Lodge (The Salvation Army), 11 Wing Sing Lane, Yau Ma Tei, Kowloon, ph 2771 9266 - 54 rooms, coffee shop, tour desk - $580-820.

Holy Carpenter Guest House, 1 Dyer Avenue, Hung Hom, Kowloon, ph 2362 0301 - 14 rooms - $640.

Caritas Lodge (Boundary St), 134 Boundary Street, Kowloon, ph 2339 3777 - 40 rooms, coffee shop, tour desk - $510-$780.

STB Hostel (HK) Ltd, 2/F Great Eastern Mansion, 255-261 Reclamation Street, Mong Kok, ph 2710 9199 - 26 rooms, tour desk - $580-630.

Chungking House, Chung King Mansion, Blk A, 4th & 5th Floor, 40 Nathan Road, Tsimshatsui, ph 2366 5362 - 82 rooms, restaurants (Cantonese, American), coffee shop, tour desk - $370-400.

Local Transport

Hong Kong has an efficient and inexpensive public transport system that includes aboveground and underground railways, ferries, trams, buses, minibuses and the ubiquitous taxis.

Traffic drives on the left, but this information is included to prevent people not used to this system from being run over, it is not a suggestion that you try to hire a car. I really feel that you have to be born in Hong Kong to think of attempting to get mixed up with the traffic. Anyway, it is a small place, there are signs in English everywhere, and it is really easy to find your way around.

The only thing to remember when using the buses and trams is that you have to have the correct fare, so it is wise to carry a fair amount of small change at all times.

Taxis

Hong Kong has over 17,000 licensed taxis, so except for rainy days and race days, there are plenty to go round. The only problem you may face is getting a driver who doesn't speak English, and this is easily solved by having someone at your hotel write your destination in Chinese characters. If you think that a taxi driver has given you a rough time, you can ring the police hotline (2527 7177), but you must have the taxi number for your complaint to be investigated.

Taxis are red on the Island and in Kowloon, and drivers tend to stick to one side or the other. Actually, they can become quite lost out of their own environment. Flag fall is HK$14.50, which includes the first 2km, then the fare is HK1.30c per quarter kilometre. Extra charges that are allowed are: HK$20 for the Cross Harbour Tunnel and the Eastern Harbour Crossing (HK$10 is for the return toll); HK$30 for the new Western Harbour Crossing; HK$6 for Lion Rock; HK$3 for Junk Bay; HK$5 for the Aberdeen Tunnel; HK$5 per piece of luggage; HK$1.30 per minute of waiting time; and HK$2 for a radio-call (booking).

A vacant taxi has a red 'For Hire' flag visible in the windscreen during the day, and at night the 'Taxi' sign on the roof is lit up. If a vacant taxi sails past ignoring your hail, it is probably because you are standing in a restricted area, such as along a road with single or double yellow lines. If their red flag is covered it usually means that they are on their way home and not interested in another fare. Often they will cover their flag with a sign saying either 'Hong Kong' or 'Kowloon' which means that they want to go back to their base, but as this is usually in Chinese, it is really only for the benefit of the locals.

Taxis are green and white in the New Territories, and blue on Lantau, and those in the New Territories only pick up and put down in the Territories (as Lantau is an island, those drivers really don't have much choice). The flag fall for these districts is HK$13 and the fare is HK$1.30c per quarter kilometre.

Trains

Above Ground (KCR)

The Kowloon-Canton Railway has two main services a day - the daily express trains for people going through to China (mentioned in the How To Get There section), and the local stopping service, which is used by commuters and visitors who want to sightsee.

Trains leave from Hung Hom in Kowloon every 10 to 15 minutes, and stop at Mong Kok, Kowloon Tong, Tai Wai, Shatin, Shatin Racecourse, Fotan, University, Tai Po Market, Tai Wo, Fanling and Sheung Shui, which is as far as you can go without a visa for China.

From Kowloon to Sheung Shui takes about half an hour, and once past Shatin, it's a very scenic trip. There's nothing much to see at Sheung Shui, but consider getting off at Tai Po Market or Fanling for a look around.

A single ordinary-class ticket from Kowloon to Sheung Shui is HK$8.50 and a first-class ticket is HK$15.50 (double for return fare), children 3-12 half fare.

Underground (MTR)

The Mass Transit Railway stretches from Central, across the harbour and up through Kowloon where it divides into two lines, one ending up at Tsuen Wan in the west and the other at Lam Tin. The Island Line, with **14 stations,** operates along the north side of Hong Kong Island.

The MTR carries around a million passengers a day, so it is obvious that peak hour is not the time for visitors to try battling their way on to these trains. At other times it is the fastest way of getting to the shopping areas on both sides of the harbour, with the most convenient stations being Central, Admiralty (at the start of Wanchai) and Tsimshatsui. The MTR operates from 6am-1am.

Fares range from HK$4 to HK$12.50, and it costs HK$11.00 to cross the harbour from either Central or Admiralty stations to Tsimshatsui. The ticketing system is electronic, and the machines take HK$5, $2, $1, 50c and 20c. You can get small change from machines nearby, but notes have to be changed at the Information Desks. The single journey ticket is valid on day of issue for one ride only, and only for 90 minutes after passing through the turnstile. **Eating, drinking and smoking is forbidden on trains and stations, and there are no public toilets on either. Large luggage is also not accepted.**

MTR/KCR Tourist Ticket
This can be purchased from the ticket offices in the MTR stations; the Hang Seng Mini-banks at Central, Admiralty, Wanchai, Causeway Bay, Tsimshatsui, Jordan, Yau Ma Tei and Kowloon Tong; and all KCR ticket offices (except Lo Wu Station) and Customer Service Centres. **The ticket costs HK$30** and is valid for use anywhere on the MTR or the ordinary class of the KCR (except Lo Wu Station). Not valid on the Airport Express. The ticket must be purchased within 14 days of arrival but you no longer have to show your passport. It is valid for 2 trips only.

> **The Ticket doesn't save you any money as the total fare value is actually HK$30, but you can end up even on the last ride because you can travel anywhere regardless of the amount remaining on the ticket.**

For example, if you have $1 remaining on the card, and undertake a journey costing say $5.90, you can still complete the trip. This is great in theory but the most expensive ride is HK$14.50 so you are paying HK$1.00 extra anyway. You even get the ticket back from the machine as a souvenir. The value of the card is that it saves having to queue to buy a ticket.

Light Rail Transit (LRT)
The LRT operates in the western New Territories within Tuen Mun, and from Tuen Mun to Yuen Long. The LRT operates

from 5.30am to 12.30am daily, fares $3.50 to $5.20. For enquiries, ph 2468 7788.

Ferries
Star Ferry
The famous green and white ferries have been travelling between Central and Tsimshatsui since 1898, and the eight minute journey across the harbour is a photographer's delight. The ferries have names such as *Twinkling Star*, *Celestial Star* and *Meridien Star* and every movie ever shot in Hong Kong has had the characters on a Star Ferry in at least one scene.

Despite the reputation, the journey is still one of the cheapest in the world at HK$2.00 first class single (upper deck), or HK$1.70 for the lower deck second class.

There is also a service from Central to Hung Hom and the Kowloon-Canton Railway terminus (HK$2.50 upper deck); and one from Tsimshatsui to Wanchai (HK$2). The Central to Tsimshatsui service operates 6.30am-11.30pm, with a three-minute frequency during peak hours. The Hung Hom service runs 7am-7.20pm, and the Tsimshatsui to Wanchai, 7.30am-11pm, ph 2366 2576.

Hong Kong Ferries
Most of the ferries in this fleet of double or triple-deckers leave from the Outlying Districts Ferry Services Pier along the waterfront in Central District, and they travel to the many outlying islands, and across the harbour. It is estimated that they carry 300,000 passengers a day, and you can save a lot of time by buying a return ticket. The various journeys average about an hour each way, and cost only a few dollars. Ferry schedules and more information can be obtained by contacting the HKTA Information and Gift Centres, or the Hong Kong Ferry (Holdings) Co, ph 2542 3081.

Trams
The Hong Kong Island tram system has been in operation for 88 years, and is popularly known as the 'pollution solution'. The trams run from Kennedy Town in the west to Shau Kei Wan in the east, and generally travel in a straight line across the north of the Island, except for some who make a small detour around Happy Valley.

This is another inexpensive form of transport, with the whole trip costing HK$1.60 (children HK80c), but remember that you have to put the exact money into a small box by the driver's seat on your way out. The trams operate daily from 6am to 1am.

A tourist attraction is the Antique Tram, complete with front and rear balconies and brass fittings, which is available for charter, or you can ride in it on the 'Tram Tour with Dim Sum'. For more information phone 2559 8918.

Peak Tram

The fully automated and computerised Peak Tram takes about five minutes for its spectacular climb 397m (1302 ft) from the lower terminus on Garden Road, behind the Hongkong Hilton Hotel, to the Peak Tower and an incredible view of Hong Kong, Kowloon and the islands of the South China Sea. **The cost is HK$18 each way for adults (HK$28 return), and HK$5 each way for children (HK$8 return), ph 2522 0922.**

A free shuttle bus service runs from the Star Ferry concourse in Central to the lower terminus on Garden Road at 20-minute intervals from 9am to 7pm daily, and the peak tram runs every 10 to 15 minutes from 7am to midnight.

I have to say that for anyone with a fear of heights, the 5 minute trip to the Peak seems to take about an hour, and is terrifying. As the tram ascends, almost vertically, the buildings you pass seem to be leaning over ready to fall at any second. So for the faint-hearted, you can take bus no 15 from the Central Bus Station in Exchange Square, or minibus no 1 from HMS Tamar near City Hall, to the top of the Peak, and be in a fit state to enjoy the view, which should not be missed.

Buses

China Motor Bus runs cream and blue double-decker buses on Hong Kong Island, and Kowloon Motor Bus has cream and red double-deckers in Kowloon. The Hong Kong Tourist Association publishes leaflets with full details of most bus routes, or call the appropriate company - CMB, ph 2565 8556, or KMB, ph 2745 4466. These are definitely not the most modern buses, in fact some of them are almost antiques, **but the fares again are very reasonable, ranging from HK$1.10 to HK$32.** Once again you pay the exact fare into a box as you enter, so make sure you have some small change.

Maxicabs

These green and yellow minibuses operate on fixed routes, with fixed **prices ranging from HK$1.50 to HK$18, depending on distance.** Examples of routes are: from Star Ferry Kowloon to Tsimshatsui East shopping area; from Star Ferry on Hong Kong Island to Bowen Road and Ocean Park.

 There is also a yellow and red minibus service, but this is more for the locals as the small English destination signs are not always visible until it is too late to hail the bus.

Helicopters

Heliservices (HK) Ltd, ph 2523 6407, operate charter flights in a French-made Squirrel, but you must charter the whole aircraft, which seats a maximum of five people, for a minimum of 30 minutes. In a single engined Squirrel a trip along the west and south coast of Hong Kong Island or flights over Lantau Island cost HK$5,440 for 30 minutes; one over the New Territories costs HK$8,160 for 45 minutes. To book phone Mrs Ela, Central Heliport, ph 2802 0200.

Car Rental

Don't even consider hiring a car. Not only is the traffic off-putting, there is a drastic shortage of parking places. If you feel that you have to travel by car, most major hotels have a fleet of chauffeur-driven cars, or they can arrange for you to hire one. It is an expensive way of getting around, though.

Rickshaws

If you have a preconceived idea of playing the idle rich and reclining in a rickshaw with your tons of shopping, while a barefoot coolie speeds you to your destination, forget it.

    They have almost completely disappeared from Hong Kong, except for a few who congregate at the Star Ferry Concourse on Hong Kong Island, and who expect to be photographed (for HK$20-50) rather than work for a living. One look will convince you that they are not exactly in peak running condition. If you persist they may reluctantly agree to take you leisurely around the block. The cost will be around HK$100.

Eating Out

Hong Kong is home to some of the finest restaurants in the world, and is internationally known as a gourmet's paradise, and the culinary capital of Asia.

Each year the Hong Kong Food Festival is celebrated, but don't worry if you are not around for that as good food and drink are available all year round.

The Hong Kong Tourist Association put out an excellent booklet entitled *Dining and Nightlife* and its 244 pages will make sure you don't go hungry, and have something to do in the evenings.

In the Accommodation section of this book you will note that every hotel has at least one restaurant, some have several with different cuisines, but there are also many restaurants that are quite independent of a hotel. To list even these would be a book in itself, so I have settled for those restaurants that offer the different Asian cuisines. After all, why go to the culinary capital of Asia and eat the same dishes that are readily available at home? If you must, then go to any of the large hotels and you will be satisfied.

The following are listed under the type of cuisine, with prices for a standard three course meal per person, not including drinks. By the way, wine is not a big thing with the Chinese, their own wine in fact tastes a bit like straight, strong, cheap, whisky.

Some restaurants offer a Western wine list. We have marked these with an asterisk.

Cantonese (Guangzhou)

This is the most popular cuisine in Hong Kong, and the one that people from other countries are most familiar with. It is renowned for its fresh, delicate flavours, and does not usually contain frozen or processed foods, although it often uses dried seafood.

Dim Sum is served in most Cantonese restaurants, and means 'light snack'. It originated as something small to eat with *Yum Cha*, or, in other words, something to eat while drinking copious amounts of tea with friends. In other countries, such as Australia for example, the tea and the snacks are known as Yum Cha, and the words 'Dim Sum' are ignored. In any case, sometimes baskets of dishes are paraded around the restaurant on trolleys and you simply point to what you want, at other venues you fill in what you want on a card and hand it to the waiter. The latter can be a problem if you do not read Chinese, unless you have a copy of the HKTA's *Your Guide to Some Dim Sum Delights in Hong Kong.* **There are usually three to four pieces per order, and each dish, plate or steamer basket has a different price, generally averaging between HK$15-40 each.** Dim Sum is also offered in some restaurants that specialise in cuisine from other regions of China.

Popular Dim Sum dishes are: Har Gau (shrimp dumpling); Siu Mai (meat dumpling); Pai Kwat (steamed spareribs); Ngau Yuk Mai (steamed beef ball); Cha Siu Bau (steamed barbecued pork bun); Chun Kuen (fried spring roll); Woo Kok (deep-fried taro rolls stuffed with vegetables); Fun Gwor (steamed dumplings with pork, shrimp and bamboo shoots); Cheung Fun (steamed rice flour rolls with barbecued pork, beef or shrimp); Jin Fun Gwor (pan-fried dumplings with pork, shrimp and bamboo shoots, served with clear broth). Some Desserts: Daan Tart, Custard Tart, and Ngor Mai Chee (sweet rice dumplings with shredded coconut).

Restaurants

HK$400+
Hong Kong Island
Fook Lam Moon Restaurant, G/F, 34-45 Johnston Road, Wanchai, ph 2866 0663 - open daily 11.30am-11.30pm; Dim Sum daily 11.30am-3pm.

Kowloon
Fook Lam Moon Restaurant, Shop A, G/F, 31 Mody Road, Tsimshatsui, ph 2366 0286 - open daily 11.30am-11.30pm; Dim Sum daily 11.30am-3pm.

Sun Tung Lok Sharks Fin Restaurant*, G/F & Mezz Floor, Sunning Plazam 1-5 Sunning Road, Causeway Bay, ph 2882 2899 - open daily 11.30am-2.30pm & 6-11pm; Dim Sim: Daily 11.30am-2.30pm.

Qiao Yuan Restaurant*, 4/F, Miramar Tower, Miramar Shopping Centre, 1-23 Kimberley Road, Tsim Sha Tui, ph 2375 2375 - open daily noon-3pm & 6-9pm; Dim Sim: daily noon-3pm.

Others in this category are at the **Hyatt Regency, Regent Hotel.**

HK$250-400

Hong Kong Island

Summer Palace*, 5/F, Island Shangri-La, Pacific Place, Supreme Court Road, Central, ph 2820 8552 - open daily 11.30-3pm, 6.30pm-11pm. Dim Sum: Daily 11.30am-3pm.

Others in this category are at the JW **Marriott Hotel, Grand Hyatt and Regal Hongkong Hotel.**

Kowloon

Chung Kong Seafood Restaurant*, Shop11-16, G/F, China Hong Kong City, 33 Canton Road, Tsim Sha Tsui, ph 2730-1388 - open daily 11am-mindnight; Dim Sum: daily 11am-3pm.

Jade Terrace Restaurant*, 2/F, Peninsula Centre, 67 Mody Road, Tsimshatsui East, ph 2311 8888 - open daily 11am-1am; Dim Sum daily 11.30am-3pm.

Spring Moon Chinese Restaurant*, Shop R1 2/F, China Hong Kong City, 33 Canton Rd, Tsimshatsui, ph 2366 6251 ext 3160 - open Mon-Sat 11.30am -3pm, 6pm-midnight, Sun & public holidays 10am-5pm, 6pm-midnight; Dim Sum Mon-Sat 11.30am-3pm, Sun and public holidays 10am-5pm.

Others in this category are at **The Royal Garden, New World Hotel, The Hongkong Hotel, Grand Stanford Harbour View Hotel Kowloon Shangri-La Hotel, Hong Kong Renaissance Hotel, Hotel Nikko and The Kowloon Hotel.**

HK$150-250

Hong Kong Island

Bamboo Village Fishermen's Wharf*, Shop Nos. 3-10, G/F, Tonnochy Towers, 350-274 Jaffe Road, Wan chai, ph 2827 1188 - open Mon-Sat 11am-5am. Sun & PH 10.30am-5am. Dim Sum:

daily 11am-3pm & 11pm-5am

*Guangzhou Garden Restaurant**, 4/F, Tower Two, Exchange Square, 8 Connaught Place, Central, ph 2525 1163 - open daily 11.30am-3pm; 6pm-midnight.

Cityplaza Harbour Restaurant, Unit 255 Cityplaza Phase 2, Taikoo Shing, Quarry Bay, ph 2884 4188 - open Mon-Fri 11am-midnight, Sat 10am-midnight, Sun and public holidays 9am-midnight; Dim Sum Mon-Fri 11am-3.30pm, Sat 10am-3.30pm, Sun and public holidays 9am-3.30pm.

*East Ocean Seafood Restaurant**, 3/F, Harbour Centre, 25 Harbour Road, Wanchai, ph 2827 8887 - open Mon-Sat 11am-midnight, Sun and public holidays (PH) 10am-midnight; Dim Sum daily 11am-6pm.

*House of Canton**, Shop 101-103, Caroline Centre, 2-38 Yun Ping Road, Causeway Bay, ph 2882 1383 - open daily 11am-midnight; Dim Sum 11am-5pm.

Luk Yu Teahouse & Restaurant, 26 Stanley Street, Central, ph 2523 5464 - open daily 7am-10pm; Dim Sum daily 7am-6pm.

*Pearl Court Restaurant**, 1/F, Shui On Centre, 8 Harbour Road, Wanchai, ph 2802 0222 - open Mon-Sat 11am-3pm, 5.30pm-11.30pm, Sun & PH 10am-11.30pm; Dim Sum daily 11am-3pm.

*Tao Yuan Restaurant**, 3/F, Great Eagle Centre, 23 Harbour Road, Wanchai, ph 2827 8080 - open Mon-Sat 11am-midnight, Sat-Sun 10am-midnight; Dim Sum Mon-Sat 11am-5pm, Sat-Sun 10am-5pm.

*Tsui Hang Village Restaurant**, 2/F, New World Tower, 16-18 Queen's Road Central, ph 2524 2012 - open Mon-Sat 11.30am-11.30, Sun and public holidays 10am-11.30pm; Dim Sum Mon-Sat 2.30-5.30pm, Sun and public holidays 10am-5.30pm.

*Windsor Palace Chinese Restaurant**, G/F and 2/F, Windsor House, 311 Gloucester Road, Causeway Bay, ph 2895 2123 - open daily 7.30am-midnight; Dim Sum daily 7.30am-3pm.

*Yung Kee Restaurant**, 36-40 Wellington Street, Central, ph 2522 1624 - open daily 11am-11.30pm; Dim Sum Mon-Sat 2-5pm, Sun & PH 11am-5pm.

Kowloon

*East Ocean Seafood Restaurant**, Basement 1, East Ocean Centre, 98 Granville Road, Tsimshatsui East, ph 2723 8128 - open

Mon-Sat 11am-midnight, Sun & PH 10am-midnight; Dim Sum daily 11am-6pm.

Flourishing Kitchen Restaurant*, Shop 29, Basement 2, New World Centre, 18-24 Salisbury Road, Tsimshatsui, ph 2369 5787 - open daily noon-11.30pm.

Flower Lounge Restaurant*, Shop 154-155 World Commerce Centre, Harbour City, 11 Canton Road, Tsimshatsui, ph 2730 2200 - open Mon-Sat 11am-midnight, Sun & PH 10am-midnight; Dim Sum daily 11am-4pm.

Fontana Restaurant*, 2/F Multifield Plaza, 3-7A Prat Avenue, Tsimshatsui, ph 2369 9898- open Mon-Sat 11am-midnight, Sun & PH 10am-midnight; Dim Sum Mon-Sat 11am-3pm, Sun & PH 10am-3pm.

North Sea Fishing Village Restaurant*, Basement 1, Auto Plaza, 65 Mody Street, Tsimshatsui East, ph 2723 6843 - open daily 11am-midnight; Dim Sum daily 11am-2.30pm.

Ocean City Seafood Restaurant*, Level 3 New World Centre, 18 Salisbury Road, Tsimshatsui, ph 2369 9688 - open Mon-Sat 8am-5pm, Sun & PH 7.30am-1am; Dim Sum Mon-Sat 8am-5pm, Sun & PH 7.30am-5pm.

Siu Lam Kung Seafood Restaurant*, 17-21 Minden Avenue, Tsimshatsui, ph 2721 6168 - open daily noon-11pm.

Tsui Hang Village Restaurant*, G/F, Mirramar Shopping Centre, 1 Kimberley Road, Tsimshatsui, ph 2368 6363 - open Mon-Sat 11.30-midnight, Sun & PH 10am-midnight; Dim Sum Mon-Sat 11.30am -5.30pm, Sun & public holidays 10am-5pm.

New Territories
Hoi Tin Garden Restaurant*, 5 Sam Shing Street, CastlePeak Bay, Tuen Mun, ph 698 1168 - open daily 7am-midnight; Dim Sum daily 7am-5pm.

Hsin Kuang Restaurant*, lvl 3, Shatin Plaza, S.T.T.L. 189, Sha Tin, ph 2698 6338 - open daily 6.30am-midnight;

4/F Nam Fung Centre, 264-298 Castle Peak Road, Tsuen Wan, ph 2498 4333 - open daily 7am-midnight.

151-159 Tai Wo Hau Road, Kwai Chung, ph 2427 3288 - open daily 6am-midnight.

Yu Wo Tong Restaurant*, G/F, 36 Main Street, Lau Fau Shan, Yuen Long, ph 2472 1155 - open daily 10am-10pm.

Other restaurants are found in the **Kowloon Panda Hotel,**

Regal Riverside Hotel, Royal Park Hotel.

Outlying Islands
Lamma Mandarin Seafood Restaurant*, No.8 G/F, First Street, Sok Kwu Wan, Lamma Island, ph 2982 8128 - open daily 10am-10pm.

Man Fung Seafood Restaurant*, 5 Main Street, Yung Shue Wan, Lamma Island, ph 2982 1112 - open daily 6am-9pm; Dim Sum daily 6am-11am.

Peach Garden Seafood Restaurant*, D.D., Lot 583, Sok Kwu Wan, Lamma Island, ph 2982 8581 - open daily 10am-11pm.

HK$150 or less
Hong Kong Island
Ah Yee Lee Tong Restaurant Ltd have a range of cafés that have dishes at this price point - all places are comfortable with 3 restaurants in **Hong Kong Island** - ph 2834 3480, ph 2573 0402, ph 2576 8385; five restaurants in **Kowloon** - ph 2366 6782, ph 2366 6782, ph 2770 1180, ph 2756 9746, ph 2723 5986; two restaurants in the **New Territories** - ph 2492 0505, ph 2673 6548; normally opened from 11.30am-midnight. They do not serve european wine.

Diamond Restaurant, 265-275 Des Voeux Road Central, ph 2544 4708 - open daily 6.30am-11pm; Dim Sum daily 6.30am-4pm.

Jade Garden Restaurant*, 1/F, Swire House, 11 Chater Road, Central, ph 2526 3031 - open Mon-Sat 11.30am-midnight, Sun and public holidays 10am-midnight; Dim Sum 2.30am-6pm, Sat 11.30am-6pm, Sun & PH 10am-6pm.

1/F Hennessy Centre, 500 Hennessy Road, Causeway Bay, ph 2895 2200 - open daily 8am-11.30pm; Dim Sum daily 8am-6pm.

Shop 5, LG/F, Jardine House, 1 Connaught Place, Central, ph 2524 5098 - open Mon-Sat 11am-3pm & 5.30pm, Sun & public holidays 10am-11.30pm; Dim Sum Mon-Sat 11am-3pm, Sun & public holidays 10am-5pm.

Jumbo Floating Restaurant*, Shuttle ferries operate from piers in Wong Chuk Hang & opp. Aberdeen Centre, Shum Wan, Aberdeen, ph 2553 9111 - open daily 7am-11pm; Dim Sum daily 7am-5pm.

*North Point Fung Shing Restaurant**, G/F and 1/F, 62-68 Java Road, North Point, ph 2578 4898 - open daily 11am-11pm, Dim Sum 11.30am-2.30pm.

*Tai Woo Restaurant**, 15-19 Wellington Street, Central, ph 2524 5618 - open Mon-Sat 10.30-midnight, Sun 10am-Midnight; Dim Sun Mon-Sat 10am-1pm, Sun 10am-4pm.

*Tung Yuen Seafood Restaurant**, 3/F, Tai Yau Building, 181 Johnston Road, Wanchai, ph 2833 6116 - open daily 10.30am-11.30pm; Dim Sum daily 10.30am-5pm.

Kowloon

*Harbour View Seafood Restaurant**, 3/F, Tsimshatsui Centre, 66 Mody Road, Tsimshatsui East, ph 2722 5888 - open Mon-Sat 11am-midnight, Sun & public holidays 9.30am-midnight; Dim Sum daily 11am-5pm.

*Jade Garden Chinese Restaurant**, 4/F, Star House, 3 Salisbury Road, Tsimshatsui, ph 2730 6888 - open daily 10am-3pm, (Sun & PH 8am-3pm) & 5.30pm to midnight;

BCC Bank Building, 25-31 Carnarvon Road, Tsimshatsui, ph 2369 8311 - open daily 7.30am-midnight. Dim Sum daily 7.30am-5pm.

Seasons Barbeque Restaurant[Boiling Pot]*, 22 Hillwood Road, Tsimshatsui, ph 2723 4609; G/F, 23 Playing Field Road, Mong Kok, ph 2381 2393; - open daily 11.30am-2am; Dim Sum daily 11.30am-2.30pm.

*Tai Woo Restaurant**, 14-16 Hillwood Road, Tsimshatsui, ph 2369 9773 - open Mon-Sat 11am-3am, Sun 10am-3am; Dim Sum daily 11am-4pm.

G/F-3/F, 20-20A Grabville Road, Tsimshatsui, ph 2739 8813 - open Mon-Sat 11am-3am, Sun 10am-3am; Dim Sum daily 11am-4pm.

New Territories

*Kar Shing Restaurant**, Room 333-348, 3/F, Yuen Long Plaza, 249-251 Castle Peak Road, Yuen Long, ph 2476 3228 - open daily 7am-11pm; Dim Sum daily 7am-3pm.

*Lung Wah Hotel Restaurant**, 22 Ha Wo Che, Shatin, ph 2691 1594 - open daily 11am-11pm.

*Sai Kung Fung Lum Restaurant**, G/F, Siu Yat Building, Sai Kung, ph 2792 6623 - open daily 11.30am-11pm.

Yucca De Lac Restaurant*, Ma Liu Shui, Shatin, ph 2691 1630 - open daily 11am-11pm.

Outlying Islands
Baccarat Restaurant*, G/F, 9A Pak She Praya Road, Cheung Chau, ph 2981 0668 - open daily 11am-11pm.

Bay-View Chinese Restaurant*, The Warwick Hotel Cheung Chau, East Bay, Cheung Chau, ph 2981 0081 - open daily noon-11pm.

Lamma Regent Seafood Restaurant*, G/F, 11-12 First Street, Sok Kwu Wan, Lamma Island, ph 2982 8385 - open daily 11am-11pm.

Peking

Hong Kong retains the name 'Peking' for this cuisine instead of the modern 'Beijing', and many of the dishes in this category come from the old Imperial courts, which obviously had their pick of the best ingredients.

Liberal use is made of stronger flavoured roots and vegetables, such as peppers, garlic, ginger, leek and coriander (Chinese parsley), and because of the region being located much further to the north, the food is more substantial to compensate for the colder climate. Where Cantonese cuisine has rice as its staple diet, Peking-style has noodles, dumplings and breads, and in some of the restaurants that specialise in these type of dishes, demonstrations are given of the art of turning a lump of dough into a skein of even-sized noodles.

The most famous dish is, of course, Peking Duck, usually prepared for a minimum of six people. The prized part of this dish is the crisp skin, which is carved off and the pieces wrapped in think pancakes with spring onions or leeks, cucumber, turnip and plum sauce. The remainder of the duck meat can be sauteed with bean sprouts, and the bones made into a soup with Tientsin cabbage. Other popular dishes are sizzling plates of seafood or meat, and beggar's chicken. This misnamed dish consists of a whole chicken stuffed with mushrooms, pickled Chinese cabbage, herbs and onions, wrapped in lotus leaves, sealed in clay and cooked slowly.

Restaurants

HK$150-250
Hong Kong Island
King Heung Restaurant*, G/F, Riviera Mansion, 59-65 Paterson Street, Causeway Bay, ph 2577 1035 - open daily noon-3pm, 6pm-11.30pm; Dim Sum daily noon-3pm (handmade noodle demonstrations).

Peking Garden Restaurant*, 1st & 2nd Basement, Alexandra House, 6 Ice House Street, Central, ph 2526 6456 - open daily 11.30am-3pm, 5.30pm-midnight;

Excelsior Plaza, East Point Road, Causeway Bay, ph 2577 7231 - open daily 11.30am-3pm, 5.30pm-midnight, Sun and public holidays 10.30am-midnight;

Unit 201, Cityplaza II, 1111 King's Road, Taikoo Shing, Quarry Bay, ph 2884 4131 - open daily 11.30am-3pm, 5.30pm-midnight, Sun and public holidays 10.30am-midnight;

Shop 003, The Mall, Pacific Place, 88 Queensway, Central, ph 2845 8452 - open daily 11.30am-3pm, 5.30pm-midnight, Sun and public holidays 10.30am-midnight.

Kowloon
Beijing Restaurant*, 34-36 Granville Road, Tsimshatsui, ph 2721 1808 - open daily 11am-11pm; Dim Sum daily 11am-5pm.

Grand Peking Restaurant*, 3/F, The Prudential Assurance Tower, 79 Chatham Road South, Tsimshatsui, ph 2311 9393 - open daily 11am-3pm, 5pm-11.30pm.

Peking Garden Restaurant*, 3/F, Star House, Tsimshatsui, ph 2735 8211 - open daily 11.30am-3pm, 5.30pm-midnight, Sun and public holidays 10.30am-midnight;

1/F, Empire Centre, 68 Mody Road, Tsimshatsui East, ph 2721 8868 - open daily 11.30am-3pm, 5.30pm-midnight, Sun and public holidays 10.30am-midnight.

Spring Deer Restaurant, 1/F, 42 Mody Road, Tsimshatsui, ph 2723 3673 - open daily noon-11pm; Dim Sum daily noon-2pm.

Under HK$100
Hong Kong Island
Hong Kong Chung Chuk Lau Restaurant*, 30 Leighton Road, Causeway Bay, ph 2577 4914 - open daily noon-11pm

(dumplings and noodles served all day).

Kowloon
North China Peking Seafood Restaurant, 2/F and 3/F, Polly Commercial Building, 21-23 Prat Avenue, Tsimshatsui, ph 2311 6689 - open daily 11am-midnight; Dim Sum daily 11am-3pm.

Peking Restaurant*, 1/F, 227 Nathan Road, Yau Ma Tei, ph 2735 1316 - open daily 11am-10pm.

Sun Hung Cheung Hing Restaurant*, 1/F, Kimberley Plaza, 45-47 Kimberley Road, Tsimshatsui, ph 2367 7933 - open daily 11am-11pm.

Szechuan

Szechuan, now called Sichuan, is the largest province in China, on the borders of Burma and Tibet, and the food from here is distinguished by the use of spices, such as star anise, fennel seed, chilli and coriander. Popular offerings are chillied bean paste and peppercorns, and there is plenty of garlic.

Simmering and smoking, rather than stir-frying, are the more common forms of preparation, ensuring that the spices are spread throughout the dishes. The specialty of the district is probably smoked duck, which is flavoured with peppercorns, ginger, cinnamon, orange peel and coriander, and then left to marinate in Chinese wine for 24 hours. Then it is steamed for two hours, then smoked over a charcoal fire containing camphorwood chips and red tea leaves. The result, as you can imagine, is not lacking in flavour. Popular ingredients are chicken, pork, river fish and shellfish, and once again, noodles or steamed bread are preferred to rice.

Restaurants

HK$150-250
Hong Kong Island
Sze Chuen Lau Restaurant*, G/F, 466 Lockhart Road, Causeway Bay, ph 2891 9027 - open daily noon-midnight.

Red Pepper Restaurant*, 7 Lan Fong Road, Causeway Bay, ph 2577 3811 - open daily noon-11.45pm.

Sichuan Garden Restaurant*, 3/F, Gloucester Tower, The

Landmark, 11 Pedder Street, Central, ph 2521 4433 - open daily 11am-3pm, 5.30pm-midnight; Shop 4, The Mall, Pacific Place, 88 Queensway, Central, ph 2845 8433 - open daily 11.30am-3pm, 5.30pm-midnight.

Kowloon
Crystal Palace Restaurant*,1/F, 16 Cameron Road, Tsimshatsui, ph 2366 1754 - open daily noon-10.30pm.
   Fung Lum Restaurant Ltd*, 1/F Polly Commerical Building, 21-23 Prat Avenue, Tsimshatsui, ph 2367 8686 - open daily 11am-11pm.
   House of Tang*, 1/F The Metropole Hotel, 75 Waterloo Road, Ho Man Tin, ph 2761 1711 ext 519 - open daily 11am-3pm, 5.30pm-11pm; Sun and public holidays 5.30pm-11pm; Dim Sum daily 11am-3pm.

Chiuchow

Chiu Chow is the coastal region around the Swatow district of eastern Guangdong province, and so naturally **seafood features prominently in the cuisine of the area.** The flavour of the seafood is usually enhanced by piquant sauces, such as tangerine jam for steamed lobsters, and broad bean paste for fish. An all time favourite is spicy goose, served with garlic and vinegar.

   Chiu Chow chefs are very skilled at vegetable carving, and a banquet is a work of art, as well as a culinary delight.

   Two other specialties of the area, both of which need an acquired taste, are shark's fin and bird's nest, but easy to take are the shellfish dishes and the wide variety of sweet dishes with pumpkin and taro.

   Served before and after every meal is Kwun Yum oolong tea, which you can make up your own mind about.

Restaurants

HK$150-250
Hong Kong Island
City Chiu Chow Hong Kong Restaurant*, 1-2/F, Allied Kajima Building, 138 Gloucester Road, Wanchai, ph 2598 4333 - open daily 11am-11pm, Dim Sum lunchtime.

Golden Island Bird's Nest Chiu Chau Restaurant*, 5/F, Causeway Bay Plaza, 489 Hennessy Road, Causeway Bay, ph 2838 6988 - open daily 11am-12.30am; Dim Sum daily 11am-12.30am.

Golden Island Bird's Nest Chiu Chau Restaurant*, 249 Des Vouex Road, Central, ph 2544 1638 - open daily 11am-12.30am; Dim Sum daily 11am-12.30am.

Harbour City Chiu Chow Restaurant*, 2/F Elizabeth House, 254 Gloucester Road, Causeway Bay, ph 2833 6678 - open daily 11am-11pm; Dim Sum daily 11am-3pm.

Kowloon
City Chiu Chow Restaurant*, 1/F East Ocean Centre, 98 Granville Road, Tsimshatsui East, ph 2723 6226 - open daily 11am-midnight; Dim Sum daily 11am-3pm.

Golden Island Bird's Nest Chiu Chau Restaurant*, 3/F and 4/F, BCC Building, 25-31 Carnarvon Road, Tsimshatsui, ph 2369 5211 - open daily 11am-midnight; Dim Sum daily 11am-midnight.

Under HK$150
Hong Kong Island
ChiuChow Garden Restaurant*, 3/F, Vicwood Plaza, 199 Des Voeux Road, Central, ph 2545 7778 - open daily 11am-3pm, 5.30pm-midnight.

- Basement, Jardine House, 1 Connaught Place, Central, ph 2525 8246 - open daily 11am-3pm, 5.30pm-midnight.

- 2/F and 3/F, Hennessy Centre, 500 Hennessy Road, Causeway Bay, ph 2577 3391 - open daily 11am-3pm, 5.30pm-midnight.

- G/F, Lippo Centre, Queensway, Central, ph 2845 1323 - open daily 11am-3pm, 5.30pm-midnight.

Golden Chiu Chow Garden Restaurant*, 2/F, Block 3, Aberdeen Centre, Chentu Road, Aberdeen, ph 2555 0388 - open 11am-11.30pm; Dim Sum daily 11am-3pm.

Kowloon
Eastern Palace Chiuchow Restaurant*, 3/F, Hongkong Hotel Shopping Arcade, Harbour City, Canton Road, Tsimshatsui, ph 2730 6011 - open daily 11.30am-3pm, 6pm-11pm. Dim Sum: daily 11.30am-3pm.

Shanghai

Shanghai is the major seaport in the estuary of the Yangtse River, and while not having a cuisine of its own, seems to have successfully refined those of the surrounding provinces. **The food is generally richer, heavier, sweeter and oilier than Cantonese.**

Preserved vegetables and pickles, and salted meats are used more in this cuisine, and specialties are lime and ginger flavoured '100-year-old' eggs, and 'hairy crab'. The crabs are jetted into Hong Kong trussed with green straw, and are seasonal - the females, treasured for their complexion-enhancing golden roe, are available in September; the males are good to eat, but don't seem to enhance anything, and are available in October. **The menus have different dumplings and breads, and noodles are served more than rice.**

Restaurants

HK$250-400
Snow Garden Restaurant, 2/F Eight Plaza, 8 Sunning Road, Causeway Bay, ph 2881 6837 - open daily noon-11.30pm.

HK$150-250
Hong Kong Island
Golden Snow Garden Restaurant*, 5/F China Resources Building, 26 Harbour Road, Wanchai, ph 2827 2200 - open daily 11am-11.30pm.

Golden Snow Garden Restaurant*, G/F Hong Kong Way Garden, 7 On Tai Street, Sheung Wan, ph 2815 8128 - open daily 11am-11.30pm; Dim Sum daily 11am-3pm, 6pm-11pm.

Shanghai Garden Restaurant*, Hutchison House, 10 Harcourt Road, Central, ph 2524 8181 - open daily 11.30am-3pm, 6pm-midnight.

Kowloon
Hong Kong Old Restaurant*, 3/F, Silvercord, 30 Canton Road, Tsimshatsui, ph 2314 4833 - open daily 11am-3pm, 5pm-midnight; Dim Sum daily.

Tien Heung Lau Restaurant, G/F, 18C Austin Avenue,

Tsimshatsui, ph 2368 9660 - open daily noon-2pm, 6-10pm.

Snow Garden Restaurant, 10/F, London Plaza, 219 Nathan Road, Yau Ma Tei, ph 2736 9188 - open daily noon-11.30pm.

Snow Garden Restaurant, Unit D, 4/F Miramar Shopping Centre, 1-23 Kimberley Road, Tsimshatsui, ph 2377 1331 - open daily noon-11.30pm.

Under HK$100
Hong Kong Island
Pu Dong Restaurant*, 3/F, Haleson Building, 1 Jubilee Street, Central, ph 2805 2038 - open daily 11am-11pm.

Kowloon
Great Shanghai Restaurant*, 26 Prat Avenue, Tsimshatsui, ph 2366 8158 - open daily 11am-11pm.

Shanghai Restaurant*, G/F, 24 Prat Avenue, Tsimshatsui, ph 2739 7083 - open daily 11am-4am; Dim Sum daily 11am-4am.

Wu Kong Shanghai Restaurant*, Basement, Alpha House, 27 Nathan Road, Tsimshatsui, ph 2366 7244 - open daily 11.30am-midnight; Dim Sum daily 11.30am-midnight.

Yap Pan Hong Restaurant*, G/F 35 Kimberley Road, Tsimshatsui, ph 2311 5078 - open daily 11am-4am.

Hunan

Hunan, the home province of Mao Tse-tung, is situated to the north of Guangdong province, and 'Hunan' means 'south of the lake'. Sometimes the cuisine is referred to as 'Xiang', after the river, and is similar to that of Szechuan only more so, with **liberal use of chilli, garlic and mustard.** Restaurants outside of the province itself, including those in Hong Kong, usually indicate on their menus whether dishes are mild, hot, or "sit near a fire extinguisher" (only joking!). Rice is the staple diet, but there are also beancurd rolls, dumplings and savoury buns.

Restaurants
There is really only one - *Hunan Garden Restaurant**, 3/F, The Forum, Exchange Square, 8 Connaught Place, Central, ph 2868 2880 - open daily 11.30am-3pm, 6pm-midnight (HK$250-400).

Taiwan

Originally called Formosa, Taiwan is an island, so as you would expect, seafood is much in evidence. The cuisine is influenced by nearby Fukienese and Chiu Chow, with a little bit of Japanese thrown in. **Sweet soy sauce is used in many popular dishes, and Taiwanese mushrooms are very popular.** Taiwanese noodle soup is less spicy than that from Szechuan, and sweet potatoes are the surprise ingredient in Taiwan's version of congee, the Chinese rice porridge, frequently chosen as an alternative to steamed rice.

Restaurants

There are two in this category.

Forever Green Taiwanese Restaurant, G/F, 93-95A Leighton Road, Causeway Bay, ph 2890 3448 - open daily noon-3pm, 6pm-6am (HK$150-250).

Forever Green Taiwanese Restaurant, G/F, BIC Centre, 18 Cheung Lok Street, Yau Ma Tei [Kowloon], ph 2332 7183 - open daily noon-3pm, 6pm-6am (HK$150-250).

Chinese Vegetarian

Thousands of years of Buddhist and Taoist beliefs have deeply rooted vegetarianism in Chinese society. Everyone in Hong Kong, and in China for that matter, believes that a vegetarian meal has great restorative values - tones the skin, cleanses the digestive system, purifies the blood and soothes the soul. As a consequence, there is a growing number of vegie restaurants in the urban areas, where alcohol is forbidden as well as meat.

The place of meat is largely taken by soya bean. The crafting of the curds into replicas of roast duck, barbecued pork, salted chicken and such, is almost an art form.

You may be surprised to notice that uncooked vegetables and salad items are rarely seen in these restaurants in Hong Kong. The Chinese believe that stir-frying is the way to go without losing any nutritional value.

Restaurants

HK$150-250
Hong Kong Island
Kung Tak Lam Shanghai Vegetarian Cuisine, G/F, Lok Sing Centre, 31 Yee Wo Street, Causeway Bay, ph 2890 3127 - open daily 11am-10pm.
   Vegi Food Kitchen, Flat B, G/F, Highland Mansion, 8 Cleveland Street, Causeway Bay, ph 2890 6660 - open daily 11am-midnight; Dim Sum daily 11am-5pm.

Kowloon
Kung Tak Lam Shanghai Vegetarian Cuisine, 1/F, Wang Send Guilding, 45 Carnarvon Road, Tsimshatsui, ph 2367 7881 - open daily 11am-11pm.

Under HK$150
Kowloon
Light Vegetarian Restaurant, Shop 1, G/F, New Lucky House, 13 Jordan Road, Yau Ma Tei, ph 2384 2833 - open daily 11am-11pm, Dim Sum daily 11am-4pm.

New Territories
Yuen Yuen General Restaurant, Yuen Yuen Institute, Sam Dip Tam, Tsuen Wan, ph 2490 9882 - open daily 11am-6pm.

Asian Restaurants

Hong Kong is, after all, part of Asia, and the many other types of cuisine are also represented. Here is a selection of these in the Under HK$150 bracket. Those dishes that are more expensive are stated.

Indian
Hong Kong Island
Ashoka Restaurant*, G/F, 57-59 Wyndham Street, Central, ph 2524 9623; G/F, Shop 1, Connaught Commercial Building, 185 Wanchai Road, Wanchai, ph 2891 8981 - open daily noon-2.30pm, 6-10.30pm.

Dragon Boats on Hong Kong harbour

Floating Restaurant

The lights of Hong Kong at dusk

Koh-I-Noor Indian Restaurant, 1/F, 103 California Entertainment Building, 24 D'Aguilar Street, Central, ph 2877 9706 - open daily 11.30am-3pm, 6-midnight.

Village Restaurant for Curry Lovers*, Basement, 57 Wyndham Street, Central, ph 2525 4117 - open Mon-Sat 11.30am-3pm, 6pm-11pm.

Kowloon
Koh-I-Noor Indian Restaurant, 1/F, 3-4 Peninsula Apartments, 16C Mody Road, Tsimshatsui, ph 2368 3065 - open daily 11am-3pm, 6-11pm.

Surya Restaurant, Lyton Building, 34-38 Mody Road, Tsimshatsui, ph 2366 9902 - open daily noon-3pm, 6pm-midnight.

Woodlands International Restaurant(Vegetarian), G/F, Mirror Tower, 61 Moody Road, Tsimshatsui East, ph 2369 3718 - open daily noon-3.30pm, 6.30-11pm.

Indonesian

$150-250
Hong Kong Island
Cinta-J Restaurant and Lounge*, Shop G-4, Malaysia Building, 69-75 Jaffe Road, Wanchai, ph 2529 6622 - open daily 11am-2am.

Cinta Restaurant and Lounge*, 1/f Shing Yip Building, 10 Fenwick Street, Wanchai, ph 2527 1199 - open daily 11am-2am.

Under $150
Kowloon
Java Rijsttafel Restaurant*, G/F, Han Hing Mansion, 38 Hankow Road, Tsimshatsui, ph 2376 1230 - open daily noon-10.30pm.

Korean

Hong Kong Island
Arirang Korean Restaurant*, Shop 1102, 11/F Food Forum, Times Square, 1 Matheson Street, Causeway Bay, ph 2506 3298 - open daily noon-3pm, 6-11pm.

Koreana Restaurant*, Kingston Mansion, 1 Paterson Street, Causeway Bay, ph 2577 5145 - open daily noon-11.30pm.

Kowloon
Arirang Korean Restaurant*, Shop 210, 2/F The Gateway, Canton Road, Tsimshatsui, ph 2956 3288 - open daily noon-3pm, 6-11pm.

Thai

Hong Kong Island
Supatra's Thai Restaurant and Longtail Bar*, G/F, 50 D'Aguilar Street, Lai Kwai Fong, Central, ph 2522 5073 - open daily noon-midnight.

Kowloon
Chaophraya Thai Restaurant*, G/F & 2/F, 440 Prince Edward Road, Kowloon City, ph 2382 6618 - open Mon-Fri 11am-3pm, 6pm-11.30pm; Sat,Sun,PH 11am-11.30pm.

Kowloon City Wong Chun Chun Thai Restaurant, G/F, 70-72 Nga Tsin Wai Road, Koowloon City, ph 2383 4680 - open daily 11am-2am.

Kowloon City Wong Chun Chun Thai Restaurant, G/F, 29-33 Lung Kong Road, Kowloon City, ph 2716 6269 - open daily 11am-2am.

Kowloon City Wong Chun Chun Thai Restaurant, G/F, 21-23 Prat Avenue, Tsimshatsui, ph 2721 00999 - open daily 11am-2am.

Vietnamese

$250-400.
Hong Kong Island
Indochine 1929*, 2/F, California Tower, Lan Kwai Fong, 30-32 D'Aguilar Street, ph 2869 7399 - open Mon-Sat noon-2.30pm, 6.30pm-10.30pm; Sun and public holidays 6.30pm-11pm.

$150-250
Kowloon
Golden Bull Vietnamese Restaurant*, 101 Ocean Centrem Harbour City, 5 Canton Road, Tsimshatsui, ph 2730 4866 - open daily noon-11.30pm.

Golden Bull Vietnamese Restaurant*, L1, 17, New World Centre, 18 Salibury Road, Tsimshatsui, ph 2369 4617 - open daily noon-11.30pm.

Others

There are also many Japanese restaurants, but, as in every country in the world, they fall into the higher price brackets. I always think you pay more for the 'cooking show' than for the food, but that is only my opinion.

I suppose no guide book is complete these days without mentioning those all-time kid's favourites (and many an adult too for a lunch time snack), **McDonald's and Kentucky Fried Chicken.** Well, they are here in force, and to give you an idea of the price range:

A Big Mac will set you back HK$10.20.

McDonald's
Hong Kong Island
Basement and G/F, Hang Cheong Building, 5 Queen's Road
   Central, ph 2522 1760.
   Shop A, LG/F, Ho Lee Commercial Building, 36 D'Aguilar Street, Central, ph 2530 3704
   Shop B225, Times Square, 1 Matheson Street, Causeway Bay, ph 2506 3281.
   Shop11, level 2, The Peak Galleria, 188 Peak Road, The Peak, ph 2849 5787.
   Basement, Yu To Sang Building, 37 Queen's Road, Central, ph 2526 3770.
   UG/F & LG/F, Sanwa Building, 30-32 Connaught Road, Central, ph 2523 4310.
   B2, Mitsukoshi Department Store, 500 Hennessy Road, Causeway Bay, ph 2890 1400
   LG/F & G/F, C.C. Wu Building, 302-308 Hennessy Road, Wanchai, ph 2893 9503.
   1/F, 46 Yee Wo Street, Causeway Bay, ph 2577 8240.
   Lido Beach Road, Repulse Bay, ph 2812 1544.

Kowloon
G/F, 21A-21B Granville Road, Tsimshatsui, ph 2369 6008.

2-4A Cameron Road, Tsimshatsui, ph 2721 4092.

Basement and G/F, Sands Building, 12 Peking Road/Hankow Road, Tsimshatsui, ph 2376 0170.

Shop 1 & 2, G/F, & Shop 8 Basement, Star House, 3 Salisbury Road, Tsimshatsui, ph 2735 6379.

Upper Basement and G/F, Hang Shing Building, 363-373 Nathan Road, Yau Ma Tei, ph 2780 4073.

Basement and 1/F, Pak Shing Building, 31-37 Jordan Road, Yau Ma Tei, ph 2332 5215.

Kowloon Park, 22 Austin Road, Tsimshatsui, ph 2317 1527.

53-55 Chatham Road, Tsimshatsui, ph 2721 2680.

G/F Good Hope Building, 612 Natham Road, Mong Kok, ph 2384 2728.

G/F Pacific Mansions, 172 Nathan Road, Tsimshatsui, ph 2367 6483.

G/F New Mandarin Plaza, 14 Science Museum Road, Tsimshatsui East, ph 2721 3590.

Shop 38, China Hong Kong City, 33 Canton Road, Tsimshatsui, ph 2736 1760.

Kentucky Fried Chicken

Hong Kong Island

G/F, 6 D'Aguilar Street, Central, ph 2524 1820.

G/F, 40 Yee Wo Street, Causeway Bay, ph 2577 6917.

28 Beach Road, Repulse Bay, ph 2812 0230.

Kowloon

2 Cameron Road, Tsimshatsui, ph 2366 2496.

G/F, 241-243 Nathan Road, Yau Ma Tei, ph 2730 7308.

Entertainment

Although Hong Kong's night life doesn't compare with places like Bangkok or Tokyo, there's still plenty to do, and something for everyone, and every pocket.

The luxurious, dare I say ostentatious, lobbies of the big hotels are transformed into lounges offering excellent service while a dinner-suited gentleman tickles the ivories of the in-house baby grand. Of course, patrons are expected to dress in a style befitting such elegance, and will be quickly removed if not suitably attired.

Several floors up in most hotels, HK$100 will get you into a noisy, though well-controlled, disco, where the inevitable records are often interspersed with live performers, and casually-dressed people gyrate to the music.

Or, visitors can venture out on the streets and head for an 'authentic' English pub complete with dart-boards, or an American-type bar, complete with Happy Hour, which should be plural because it usual extends for at least two, and sometimes three, hours.

Then there are the cultural centres, cinemas, night markets, nightlife tours, etc, and you may think, what is missing? Casinos! Gambling is illegal in Hong Kong, except on horse races, which may explain why they are so popular.

Newer areas such as Pacific Place in Admiralty and Times Square in Causeway Bay offer plenty of entertainment from high tech cinemas to bars, restaurants and the occasional club.

Bars and Pubs

The Karaoke Bars are very popular in this part of the world, and almost every venue will have private rooms or something much larger where the vocal cords of those of us who have not made it and want to 'holler' can indulge.

Hong Kong Island

The Admiral's Bar, City Garden Hotel, 9 City Garden Road, 231

Electric Road, North Point, ph 2887 2888 - open Sun-Thurs 4pm-1am, Fri-Sat 4pm-2am - full meals and snacks, dance floor, live music.

Bull & Bear, G/F, Hutchison House, Harcourt Road, Central, ph 2525 7436 - open Mon-Sat 11am-1am - British-style pub with darts and beer, local favourite.

Captain's Bar, Mandarin Oriental Hong Kong, 5 Connaught Road, Central, ph 2522 0111 - open daily 11am-2am - live music, night club atmosphere.

Champagne Bar, Grand Hyatt Hotel, 1 Harbour Road, Wanchai, ph 2588 1234 - open daily 5pm-2am - live entertainment, choice of champagnes by the glass.

Chinnery Bar, Mandarin Oriental Hotel, 5 Connaught Road, Central, ph 2522 0111 ext.4003- open daily 11am-9pm - colonial atmosphere, with gourmet snacks.

Cyrano, 56/F, Island Shangri-La, Pacific Place, Supreme Court Road, Central, ph 2820 8591 - open Sun-Thurs 6pm-1.30am, Fri & Sat and public holidays eve 6pm-2.30am - It is on the 56th Floor so you are pretty high, great jazz, and luxurious setting.

Dickens Bar, Excelsior Hotel, 281 Gloucester Road, Causeway Bay, ph 2837 6782 - open Sun-Thurs 11am-2am, Fri-Sat and public holidays 11am-3am - basement bar with live music and light snacks.

Harlequin Bar, Mandarin Oriental Hotel, 5 Connaught Road Central, ph 2522 0111 - open daily 11am-1am - rooftop cocktail bar, glamorous, good views.

Hideaway Bar, Grand Plaza Hotel, 2 Kornhill Rd, Quarry Bay, ph 2886 0011 - daily 5pm-1am - cocktail lounge and music bar.

JJ's Hong Kong, Grand Hyatt Hong Kong, 1 Harbour Road, Wanchai, ph 2588 1234 - open Sun-Thurs 6pm-2am, Fri-Sat and public holidays 6pm-3am - a total entertainment venue that includes a discotheque, live entertainment, pool table, darts and a pizzeria lounge.

Joe Bananas, G/F, Shiu Lam Building, 23 Luard Road, Wanchai, ph 2529 1811 - open Mon-Thurs 11am-4am, Fri-Sat 11am-6am, Sun and public holidays 8am-5am - cafe-pub, dancing area, DJ, meal-sized snacks.

Lau Ling Bar, Hotel Furama Kempinski Hong Kong, 1 Connaught Road Central, ph 2842 7506 - open Sun-Fri 9am-1am, Sat 9am-2am - popular bar, live music.

Lobby Lounge Bar, Marriott Hotel, Pacific Place, 88 Queensway, Central, ph 2841 3846 - open daily 11am-2am - largest open-plan bar counter, pianist.

Mad Dogs, 33 Wyndham Street, Central, ph 2810 1000 - open Sun-Thurs 11am-4am, Fri-Sat 11am-5am - pub meals, range of beers, wines and spirits, live bands, Trivial Pursuit nights, British football on Saturdays.

Wine Room, Furama Kempinski Hotel, 1 Connaught Road Central, ph 2842 7504 - open Mon-Sat 11.30am-3pm, 5-11pm, Sun 5pm-11pm - anteroom for the Rotisserie, club-like, quiet haven, up to 16 different wines sold by the glass.

Kowloon

Bar City, Basement 2, 22B New World Centre, Salisbury Road, Tsimshatsui, ph 2369 8571 - open daily 9pm-2.30am - complex of three entirely different bars - Zodiac, Hi tech disco; Crazy Horse Saloon, Las Vegas-style pub; Country & Western, cabaret artists.

Baron's Tavern, Holiday Inn Golden Mile Hotel, 46-52 Nathan Road, Tsimshatsui, ph 9369 3111 - open daily noon-3pm, 5pm-1am - cocktail lounge adjacent to Baron's Table Restaurant.

Bonker's Bar, Windsor Hotel, 39-43A Kimberley Road, Tsimshatsui, ph 2739 5665 extn 2267 - open Mon-Fri 4.30pm-1am, Sat 4.30pm-2am - cocktail bar and music lounge.

Chin Chin Bar, Hyatt Regency Hotel, 67 Nathan Road, Tsimshatsui, ph 2311 1234 extn 865 - open daily 11am-2am - live entertainment in the evening.

Club Bottoms Up, Basement, 14-16 Hankow Road, Tsimshatsui, ph 721 4509 - open daily 4pm-3am - one of Hong Kong's most famous nightspots. Hostess Club though the atmosphere is not men only. Enjoyable place for couples.

Great Wall Bar, Sheraton Hong Kong Hotel and Towers, 20 Nathan Road, Tsimshatsui, ph 2369 1111 extn 3277 - open daily 7am-1am - two-sectioned bar lounge with dance floor.

Inn Bar, Holiday Inn Golden Mile Hotel, 46-52 Nathan Road, Tsimshatsui, ph 2369 3111 - open daily 11am-1am - casually elegant, good inexpensive carvery luncheon.

Le Rendezvous, Regal Meridien Hotel, 71 Mody Road, Tsimshatsui East, ph 2313 8748 - open daily 4pm-2am - early-French style music bar with live band in the evening.

Middle Row Bar, Kowloon Hotel, 19-21 Nathan Road, Tsimshatsui, ph 2369 8698 - open daily 7.30am-2am - three dining and drinking venues with large glass walls overlooking the sidewalks.

Music Room, Kowloon Shangri-la Hotel, 64 Mody Road, Tsimshatsui East, ph 2721 2111 extn 8916 - open daily 5pm-2am - glass-partitioned nooks provide good conversation areas in the early evening, then a disco takes over later.

Nathan's, Hyatt Regency Hotel, 67 Nathan Road, Tsimshatsui, ph 2311 1234 extn 308 - open daily 7am-1am - piano bar, ideal for drinks before or after dinner.

Ned Kelly's Last Stand, 11A Ashley Road, Tsimshatsui, ph 2366 0562 - open daily 11.30am-2am. An 'Australian' pub featuring jazz nightly, and serving Aussie stews, sandwiches and burgers(!).

Rick's Cafe, Basement, Enterprise Centre, 4 Hart Avenue, Tsimshatsui, ph 2367 2939 - open daily 3pm-3am - predictably *Casablanca*-inspired, serves seafood and somewhat out-of-character Mexican snacks, and features many of Hong Kong's best-known musicians.

Sky Lounge, Sheraton Hong Kong Hotel and Towers, 20 Nathan Road, Tsimshatsui, ph 2369 1111 extn 4 - open Sun-Thurs 4pm-1am, Fri-Sat 4pm-2am - An elegant lounge from which you can see the sunset over Victoria Harbour with live entertainment.

Tartan Bar, Marco Polo Hotel, Canton Road, Tsimshatsui, ph 2113 7935 - open daily 11am-2am - a lobby bar with Dickensian sketches, relaxing.

The Tavern, Prince Hotel, Harbour City, Canton Road, Tsimshatsui, ph 2113 6050 - open daily 4pm-1am - Victorian decor, live music in the evenings.

Trop-East Bar & Lounge, Ramada Hotel Kowloon, 73-75 Chatham Road, Tsimshatsui, ph 2311 1100 extn 656 - open daily noon-2am - decor of an intimate movie set, exotic cocktails and strolling minstrels.

Terrace Bar, Hotel Nikko, 72 Mody Street, Tmshatsui East, ph 2739 1111 - open daily 4pm-1.30am - English pub complete with dartboard and pub food.

New Territories
Carnival Bar, Regal Riverside Hotel, Tai Chung Kiu Road,

Shatin, ph 2649 7878 extn 1280- open daily 4pm-1.30am - colourful bar with Hong Kong's first all-female band.

Lounges

Hong Kong Island
Clipper Lounge, Mandarin Oriental, 5 Connaught Road, Central, ph 2522 0111 - open daily 7.30am - 11.30pm - Soft music from 4pm on, popular rendezvous spot.

Oasis Lounge, 8/F, New World Harbour View, 1 Harbour Road, Wanchai, ph 2802 8888 extn 6353 - open Mon-Fri noon-2.30pm & 5pm-1am, Sat, Sub & PH 5pm-2am - live entertainment every evening, late-night snack menu.

Starlight Lounge, 28/F, South Pacific Hotel, 23 Morrison Hill Road, Wanchai, ph 2572 3838 extn 1454 - open daily 5pm-1am, live entertainment (filipino) every evening, late snack menu.

Kowloon
The Balcony, Royal Garden Hotel, 69 Mody Road, Tsimshatsui East, ph 2722 2033 - open daily noon-midnight- Mon-Sat lunch buffet noon-2.30pm, lounge bar serving exotic cocktails.

The Flying Machine, Regal Airport Hotel, Sa Po Road, Kowloon City, ph 2718 0333 - open daily 3pm-1am - live music and disco tracks.

The Boundary Lounge, Newton Hotel Kowloon, 58 Boundary Street, Mong Kok, ph 2787 6866 - open daily 11am-1am - comfortable lounge with great views on the old border of China and Kowloon. It has a resident keyboard player and singer.

Grammy's Lounge, G/F & 1/F, Supreme House, 2A Hart Avenue, Tsimshatsui, ph 2368 3833 - open Mon-Sat 4.30pm-6am, Sun 6pm-6am - lively cocktail and music lounge with local entertainers, for night owls.

Sky Lounge, Sheraton Hong Kong Hotel & Towers, 20 Nathan Road, Tsimshatsui, ph 2369 1111 extn 4 - open Sun-Thurs 11am-1am, Fri-Sat and public holidays 11am-2am - roof-top with glass walls and non-stop musical entertainment.

Sky Lounge, Hotel Nikko, 72 Mody Road, Tsimshatsui East, ph 2739 1111 - open daily 4pm-2am - private seating areas with harbour views.

Tiara Lounge, Kowloon Shangri-La Hotel, 64 Mody Road,

Tsimshatsui East, ph 2721 2111 - open daily 5pm-2am - sophisticated atmosphere with harbour views.

Night Clubs and Discos

In Central, Lan Kwai Fong is perhaps the best known place for clubs. This L shaped cobblestone lane is home to jazz clubs and bars of which only a few are listed here.

Many of the hotels have both nightclubs and discos on the premises. Generally the hostess nightclubs are male domains and many can provide a 'lady' for the night. I have not bothered to include these.

Hong Kong Island

The Nightingale Karaoke, The Charterhouse, 209-219 Wan Chai Road, Wanchai, ph 2833 5566 extn 1522 - open daily 4pm-2am, Fri & Sat 4pm-3pm - 16 private karaoke rooms with all sorts of modcons to help you think your voice is okay. Discs in 6 languages and snacks and drinks served..

California, G/F, California Tower, 24 Lan Kwai Fong, Central, ph 2521 1345 - open Mon-Sat noon-1am (dancing Wed, Fri, Sat), Sun 5pm-1am - American-style restaurant with disco bar in the late evening.

Nineteen 97, UG/F, 8-11 Lan Kwai Fong, Central, ph 2810 9333 - Post 97 open 24 hours, 7 days;

Mecca 97 open daily noon-2.30pm, 7-10.30pm;

National 97 open daily 11pm-5am - three venues at one site offering a cafe-restaurant (Post 97), a Middle Eastern and Mediterranean restaurant (Mecca 97) and a disco (Nation 97).

Kowloon

The Falcon, Royal Garden Hotel, 69 Mody Road, Tsimshatsui East, ph 2733 2025 - restaurant open daily noon-9.30pm; disco Sun-Thurs 9pm-2am, Fri-Sat and public holidays 9pm-3am - entertainment and disco on two levels.

Ocean City Restaurant and Night Club, Level 3, New World Centre, 18 Salisbury Road, Tsimshatsui, ph 2369 9688 - open daily 8am-1am - Las Vegas-style setting with internationally known cabaret artists. Restaurant has Cantonese cuisine.

Ocean Palace Restaurant and Night Club, 4/F, Ocean Centre, Harbour City, Canton Road, Tsimshatsui, ph 2730 7111 - open daily 7.30am-2am - Chinese classical dance show every evening, then cabaret shows and dancing to a live band. Restaurant has Cantonese cuisine.

New Territories

Cosmos Discotheque, Regal Riverside Hotel, Tai Chung Kiu Road, Shatin, ph 649 7878 - open daily 9pm-3am - full-on disco with laser beams and artificial thunderstorms for the high-energy ragers.

Performing Arts

Chinese Opera is definitely not everybody's cup of cha, but it is extremely popular with the locals, to the extent that performances are usually booked out well in advance, making it impossible for visitors to obtain tickets. If attending a performance is on your list of things to do before you leave this world, ask your travel agent, when you first make your travel plans, to arrange for tickets at either Ko Shan Theatre or Lai Chi Kok's Paladium Opera House. He can probably do this through your chosen hotel, or through the HKTA.

Highlights on the Performing Arts calendar are the Hong Kong Arts Festival, held over a month early in the year; the Hong Kong International Film Festival, usually in April; and the biennial Festival of Asian Arts, staged in the autumn.

For details of performances during your stay, pick up a copy of the Urban Council's free monthly brochure, *City News*, available at City Hall and the Arts Centre. If you have trouble contacting any of the venues listed below phone the Hong Kong Tourist Association information line , ph 2807 6177.

City Hall, near Star Ferry Pier, ph 2921 2840 (1-9pm daily): the Low Block main auditorium is a 1500-seat balconied concert hall, then there is a 470-seat theatre used for plays and chamber music. The large lobby doubles as the interval bar.

Hong Kong Arts Centre, Wanchai waterfront, ph 2582 0230 (10am-8pm daily): Shouson Theatre, Studio Theatre and Recital Hall combine to host the Arts Festival and other international presentations, but are mainly for Hong Kong's amateur and professional companies.

Hong Kong Academy for Performing Arts, opposite the HK Arts

Centre, ph 2584 8500 (Mon-Fri 8.30am-6pm, Sat 8.30am-1.30pm): the centre is an institution for vocational training in the performing arts. The Theatre Block contains six venues, including the Lyric Theatre, Drama Theatre, Orchestral Hall and Recital Hall.

Fringe Club, Lower Albert Road, Central, ph 2521 7251: a licensed, cultural club with experimentation in music, comedy, dance and drama. It's a relaxed place, and well worth temporary membership of HK$10 for one night or HK$30 for one month.

Queen Elizabeth Stadium, near Happy Valley racetrack, ph 2575 6793 (Mon-Fri 8am-9pm, Sat 8am-4pm): a 3500-seat multi-purpose arena which often has musical shows.

Hong Kong Coliseum, near Hung Hom railway terminus, Tsimshatsui East, ph 2765 9233 (11am-6.30pm daily): an inverted pyramid-shaped arena ideal for shows and sporting events that can seat 12,500.

Hong Kong Cultural Centre, near Kowloon Star Ferry Pier, ph 2734 2009 (9am-10pm daily): has three venues which offer opera, ballet and experimental theatre.

Ko Shan Theatre, near Kowloon City, ph 2334 2331 (Mon-Fri 9am-5pm, Sat 9am-1pm): a converted quarry site has become Hong Kong's first open-air theatre, suited for Chinese opera, variety shows and major film screenings.

Academic Community Hall, Baptist College, near Kowloon Tong MTR station, ph 2338 6121 (Mon-Fri 9am-5pm, Sat 9am-1pm): is often the venue for pop concerts.

Shopping

Hong Kong is a shopper's paradise, not only because it is virtually one gigantic mall, but as it is a duty-free port, no duties are levied on imported goods, except for alcohol, tobacco, perfumes, cosmetics and some petroleum products. And, compared to other countries, the duty even on these goods is minimal. Also, there is no sales tax.

Shopping here can be an exciting experience, or it can be a nightmare, especially for people who are not familiar with bargaining, which is 'compulsory' except in department stores and designer boutiques. The range of goods available is incredible, and in fact, it would be hard to think of something that is not procurable in the colony. You can literally 'shop till you drop' and you still probably won't have covered half of the stores.

Important Advice for Shoppers

As is the case everywhere in the world, things are not as cheap in Hong Kong as they once were, so comparison-shopping is a must. Don't leave this until you arrive if you are after expensive electronic or photographic equipment, rather check out the prices at home, make yourself familiar with the current exchange rate, check whether guarantees are worldwide or valid only in Hong Kong, and work out whether it is worth the bother of getting the goods home.

It is well to keep in mind too, that the general practice in Hong Kong is that goods sold are not returnable or refundable, and that deposits paid are not refundable. When ordering custom-made goods, a deposit of not less than 50% is usually required, so don't change your mind when you see something that is maybe more appealing. Once you have decided to have that stunning suede or leather outfit, or that incredible pair of shoes, custom-made, turn a blind eye to establishments offering similar goods, and concentrate on other purchases.

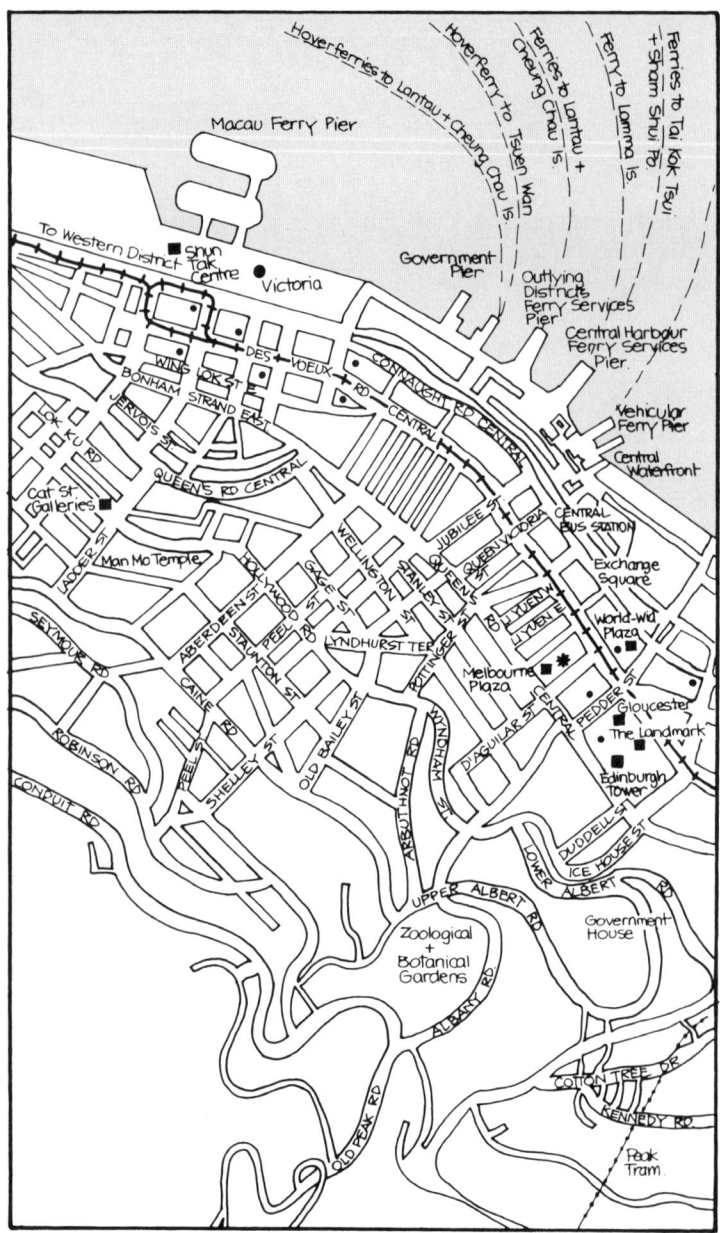

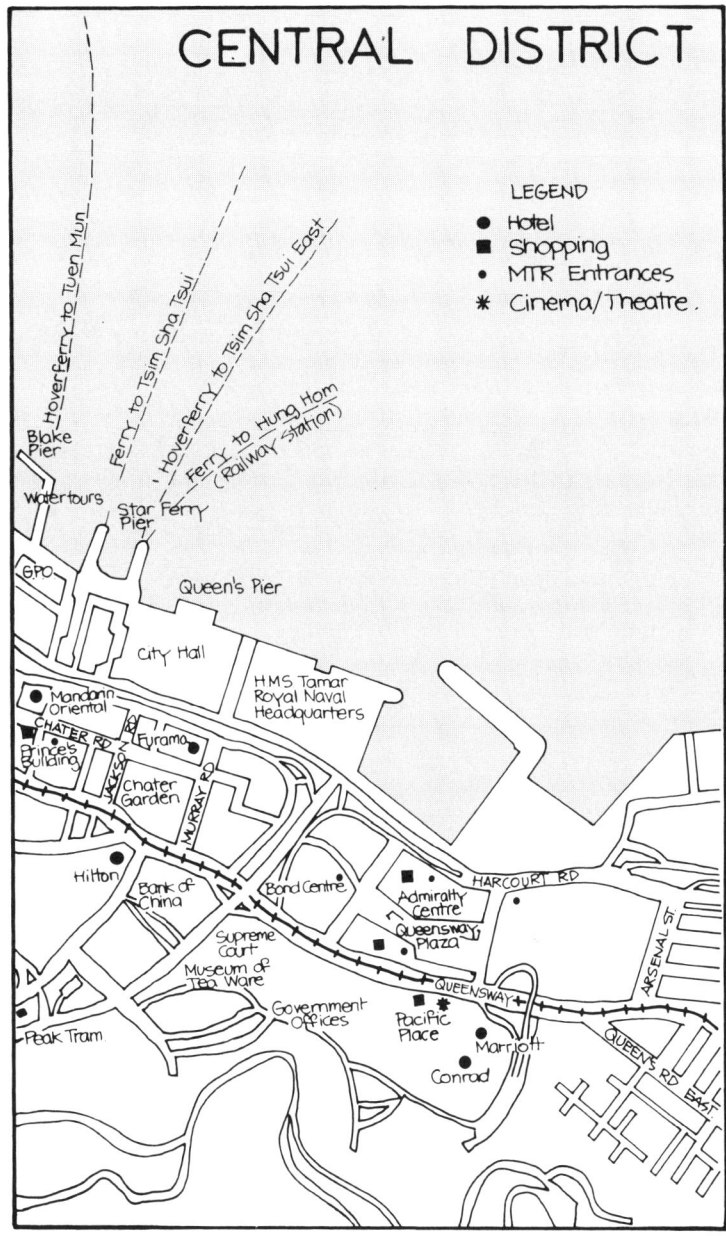

Attitude to Credit Cards

If you are going to do some serious shopping for a variety of goods, souvenirs, antiques, artifacts, etc, don't leave home with loose change and your fantastic plastic. Apart from the fact that you can get a better price if paying with real money, some establishments do not accept credit cards, and others want to add on the 6% charge, after you have exhausted yourself bargaining for a realistic price.

Bargaining

Now we are back to the subject of bargaining. It is possible to engage in this necessary evil and still maintain harmonious relations between east and west. Some westerners, however, become obnoxious and embarrassing in their efforts to browbeat what might be just an honest trader trying to make a living.

There is no need to be offensive, or to denigrate either the object or the seller, in an attempt to make a fabulous bargain you can brag about at parties for years to come.

There are, of course, *no hard and fast rules*, but remember not to look as if your life depends on you owning the article in question, and bear in mind that the local trader has loads of experience in this area. As with most things in life, a smile and a cheerful disposition will go a long way towards achieving your goal, so remember that you can catch more flies with honey than with vinegar.

Even so, it is a good idea to always shop at establishments displaying the red junk logo of the Hong Kong Tourist Association, which means that these establishments are members of the Association, and you have some rights to complain if you think you have been unfairly treated.

The HKTA put out a booklet, simply called *Shopping*, which lists its members in alphabetical order under the headings of Arts and Crafts - antiques and works of art, art galleries, ivory, Consumer Electronics - audio and video equipment and accessories, cameras and photographic equipment, photographic services, computers, electrical and electronic equipment, Clothing and Furs, Custom Tailors, Furniture, Home Decorative and Household Products - carpets and rugs, ceramics, bone china and porcelain, furniture, Jewellery and Watches, Leather Goods, Optical Goods.

The booklet also lists the sole agents for the well-known brands, eg the agent for Sanyo is Tatt Sing Sanyo Electric Co, ph 2524 5114; that for Royal Albert China is Royal Doulton HKJ Ltd, ph 2523 3361; IBM Computers have IBM China/HK Corporation ph 2825 6222. A phone call to the agent will let you know what price you can expect to pay, and where to find a reputable dealer.

Most shops are open seven days a week, except during the Chinese New Year holidays when many close for two or three days.

The hours, generally speaking, are:
Hong Kong Island
  Central and Western - 10am-6pm.
  Causeway Bay and Wanchai - 10am-9.30pm.
Kowloon
  Tsimshatsui East - 10am-7.30pm.
  Tsimshatsui, Yau Ma Tei and Mong Kok - 10am-9pm.
  The department stores in Causeway Bay are open daily, except Daimaru (closed on Wednesday) and Matsuzakaya (closed Thursday).

If you intend to buy large articles of furniture, or the like, and have them shipped home, you should check with your local customs department regarding import duties and regulations, or if you forget to do that, contact your Consulate or Trade Commission in Hong Kong. Many shops will handle the packing and shipping, and can arrange insurance. It is best to take out All Risks insurance, which covers damage in transit as well as loss. If you intend to pay with a credit card, it is worthwhile finding out if your card offers automatic insurance.

For not-so-large items, you can arrange to post them home, and some hotels offer a parcel and wrapping service. You can get full information on postal rates and maximum weights at any post office in Hong Kong, or contact the Post Office

Enquiry Bureau, ph 2921 2222, open Mon-Fri 9am-5pm, Sat 9am-1pm. Here again it is advisable to take out insurance, and to register the article.

Experienced travellers (or shoppers) usually arrive in Hong Kong with an empty suitcase packed inside another, but you have to be careful about excess baggage charges on the way home, so keep the postal option in mind.

Where to Shop

The best advice anyone can give is: **shop only at HKTA member stores**. As a condition of membership, these stores have to offer good value for money, accurately represent the products sold, and rectify justified complaints. The Association is the official, government-sponsored body representing the entire tourism industry in Hong Kong, and members are charged an annual fee to help meet administrative costs. If you have any comments or questions about a member of the Association, you are invited to contact the Membership Department on 2807 6177 (Mon-Fri 9am-5pm, Sat 9am-1pm).

I am not about to say that all shops that don't belong to the HKTA will try to 'rip you off', but you do run the risk of buying, for example, an expensive, well-known brand watch case, with inferior, local works, the original innards having been sold separately. You could also find yourself the proud owner of a handbag with a genuine-looking, instantly-recognisable designer logo, that falls apart before you board your return flight. Similar things can happen with cameras and electronic equipment, and, if you are in the market for Chinese antiques, bear in mind that there are several legitimate factories

in Hong Kong where people make hundreds of 'antiques' day after day. The factories may be legitimate, but what is a new antique worth?

All jewellers in Hong Kong are required by law to stamp their gold products with the accurate gold content, such as 18ct or 18K, but all HKTA member jewellers also stamp the shop's identity mark, which is a double guarantee of quality.

Shopping Areas

Nathan Road, Tsimshatsui

It runs from the harbour to the border of the New Territories, a distance of about 4km, and together with its side streets, such as Granville Road and Kimberley Street, has the greatest concentration of shops, department stores and arcades, and factory outlets.

Central

Hong Kong Central rivals Tsimshatsui in size and shops. For antiques and carpets, head for Hollywood Road and Wyndham Street above the Central District, and near there check out Wing On Street, popularly known as Cloth Alley, for tailors and fabrics. Arts and Crafts shops are also found in the Hollywood Road/Lok Ku Road area. Central also contains many designer boutiques at The Landmark, Gallerie and Designer boutiques. Man Wah Lane is famous for its carvers of Chinese chops, and the lanes of Li Yuen Street East and West contain stalls where you can try your bargaining techniques. Pottinger Street is the place for Haberdashery, and in Theatre Street you will find engravers and others of their ilk.

Causeway Bay

Located on Hong Kong Island, Causeway Bay is another large shopping area, although many shops here cater more for the locals. The range of goods offered, though, is extensive. Jardine's Crescent, which mainly has clothing, and Jardine's bazaar, good for dry foodstuffs, are situated here.

Happy Valley

Near the racecourse, it is a venue for shoe and handbag shops, and is easily reached by tram. The main streets here are Leighton Road and Wong Nai Chung Road.

If you like to do your *shopping under one roof,* Hong Kong has a few large shopping complexes that will fit the bill: **Harbour City, Canton Road, Tsimshatsui,** next to the cruise liner dock and near the Star Ferry Terminal, is the largest, and includes Ocean Terminal, Ocean Galleries and Ocean City, with 600

CLOTHING SIZES AND CONVERSION CHART

WOMEN'S CLOTHING
Coats, Skirts, Dresses, Slacks, Jerseys, Pullovers, etc.

Aust./N.Z.	8	10	12	14	16	18						
Europe	38	40	42	44	46	48						
United Kingdom	8	10	12	14	16	18						
United States	6	8	10	12	14	16						

Shoes

Aust./N.Z.	4	5	5½	6	6½	7	7½	8	8½	9	9½	10
Europe	34	36	37	37	38	38	39	39	40	40	41	41
United Kingdom	3	3½	4	4½	5	5½	6	6½	7	7½	8	8½
United States	4½	5	5½	6	6½	7	7½	8	8½	9	9½	10

MEN'S CLOTHING
Suits, Coats, Trousers, Jerseys, Pullovers

Aust./N.Z.	14	16	18	20	22	24
Europe	46	48	50	52	54	56
United Kingdom	36	38	40	42	44	46
United States	36	38	40	42	44	46

Shirts (Collar Sizes)

Aust./N.Z.	15	15½	16	16½	17	17½
Europe (cm)	38	39	41	42	43	44
United Kingdom	15	15½	16	16½	17	17½
United States	15	15½	16	16½	17	17½

Shoes

Aust./N.Z.	8	9	10	11	12	13
Europe	42	43	44	46	47	48
United Kingdom	8	9	10	11	12	13
United States	8½	9½	10½	11½	12½	13½

shopping outlets; **New World Centre,** adjacent to the Regent Hotel, Tsimshatsui, on the shore line; **New Town Plaza** in Shatin, New Territories; and **Taikoo Shing City Plaza,** on Hong Kong Island at the Taikoo MTR station.

Cityplaza Shopping Centre, Taikoo Shing, 1111 King's Road, Quarry Bay - ph 2567 0441.

The Mall at Pacific Place, One Pacific Place, 88 Queensway, Central - ph 2844 3888.

World Trade Centre, 280 Gloucester Roiad, Causeway Bay, ph 2576 3586.

Also in Kowloon are the Dragon Centre, 37K yen Chow Street, Sham Dhui Po - ph 2360 0982, and the Sun Arcade, 28 Canton St, Tsimshatsui - ph 2375 1203.

Department Stores

The first-time visitor to Hong Kong probably expects department stores to be like the ones at home - large, multi-storeyed buildings devoted wholly and solely to offering merchandise. In Hong Kong, the term 'department store' is actually more literal, and means that the store is divided into departments which offer different types of goods, as opposed to a jewellery store, for example, which sells just that - jewellery. The only western-style department stores are those run by Lane Crawford Ltd.

Remember, there is no bargaining in department stores.

Hong Kong Island

CRC Department Store Ltd, 31 Yee Wo Street, Causeway Bay, ph 2890 8321; 488-500 Hennessy Rd, Causeway Bay, ph 2577 0222.

Chiao Shang Building, 92-104 Queen's Rd Central, ph 2524 1051.

The Dragon Seed Co Ltd, 39 Queen's Rd Central, ph 2524 2016.

Hong Kong Daimaru Department Store Ltd, Great George Street, Causeway Bay, ph 2576 7321.

Hong Kong Matsuzakaya Co Ltd, Hang Lung Centre, 2-20 Paterson Street, Causeway Bay, ph 2890 6622.

Lane Crawford (Hong Kong) Ltd, 70 Queen's Road, Central, ph 2526 6121; G/F and Basement, Windsor House, Gloucester Road, Causeway Bay, ph 890 9533. Levels 1-3, The Mall, One Pacific Place, 88 Queensway, Central, ph 2845 1838.

Marks & Spencer P.L.C., Shop 100 & 217, Cityplaza 1, 1111 King's Road, Quarry Bay, ph 2567 2102; Shop 120 & 229, The Mall, Pacific Place Two, 88 Queensway, Central, ph 2523 2366.

Mitsukoshi Enterprises Co Ltd, Hennessy Centre, 500 Hennessy Road, Causeway Bay, ph 2576 5222.

The Sincere Co Ltd, 173 Des Voeux Rd Central, ph 2544 2688.

Sogo Hong Kong Co Ltd, East Point Centre, 555 Hennessy Road, Causeway Bay, ph 2833 8338.

Stanley Chinese Products Co Ltd, 22-26 Stanley Main Street, Stanley, ph 2813 0649.

Uny (HK) Co Ltd, Cityplaza II, 18 Taikoo Shing Road, Quarry Bay, ph 2885 0331.

Wing On Department Stores (HK) Ltd, 211 Des Voeux Road Central, ph 2852 1888; 26 Des Voeux Road Central, ph 2524 7171; Cityplaza 1, Taikoo Shing, 1111 King's Road, Quarry Bay, ph 2885 7588.

Yue Hwa Chinese Products Emporium Ltd, 278-288 King's Road, North Point, ph 2808 1363.

Kowloon

Cheong Hing Store Ltd, G/F, 72 Nathan Road, Tsimshatsui, ph 2739 6301.

CRC Department Store Ltd, Tower 1, Argyle Centre, 65 Argyle Street, Mong Kok, ph 2395 3191.

Chung Kiu Chinese Products Emporium Ltd, 47-51 Shan Tung Street, Mong Kok, ph 2780 2331; 528-532 Nathan Road, Yau Ma Tei, ph 2780 2351.

The Dragon Seed Boutique, Level 2, New World Centre, 18-24 Salisbury Road, Tsimshatsui, ph 2721 3980.

Duty Free Shoppers International Ltd, G/F-1/F, Chinachem Golden Plaza, 77 Mody Road, Tsimshatsui East, ph 2311 3813; F9-11, 1/F, Hankow Centre, 5 Hankow Road Tsimshatsui, ph 2721 2281; Shop 120B, Ocean Terminal Harbour City, 3 Canton Road, Tsimshatsui, ph 2735 5111; Shop 20, 1/F, China Hong Kong City, China Ferry Terminal, Canton Road, Tsimshatsui, ph 2736 0608; and the new international terminal.

Friendship Stores Ltd, D-F, G/F, 86-99 Canton Road, Tsimshatsui, ph 2369 8202.

Hong Kong Tokyu Department Store Co Ltd, New World Centre, 18-24 Salisbury Road, Tsimshatsui, ph 2722 0102.

Lane Crawford Ltd, Shop 100 Ocean Terminal Harbour City, 3

Canton Road, Tsimshatsui, ph 2730 2393.

Marks and Spencer PLC, 102 and 254 Ocean Centre Harbour City, Canton Road, Tsimshatsui, ph 2730 3163.

Railway Duty Free, Presales Counter, Platform 1, KCR Station, Mong Kok; Shop 7-8, Palm Mansions, Whampoa Garden, Baker Street, Hung Hom; Shop 1 and 2, KCR Station Concourse, Hung Hom, ph 2365 6071; Presales Counter, Platform 1, KCR Station, Kowloon Tong.

The Shui Hing Co Ltd, 664 Nathan Road, Mong Kok, ph 2398 3836.

The Sincere Co Ltd, 83 Argyle Street, Mong Kok, ph 2394 8233.

The Wing On Department Stores Ltd, Wing On Plaza, 62 Mody Road, Tsimshatsui East, ph 2723 2211; Shops G21-28 & B10-B15, Site11, Whampoa Garden, 6 Tak Hong Street, Hung Hon, ph 2356 4888.

Yaohan Department Store (HK) Ltd, Site 5-6, G/F and 1st Basement, Whampoa Garden, Hung Hom, ph 2766 0338.

Yue Hwa Chinese Product Emporium Ltd, 301-309 Nathan Road, Yau Ma Tei, ph 2384 0084; Basement, Mirador Mansion, 54-64 Nathan Road, Tsimshatsui, ph 2368 9165; Park Lane Shopper's Boulevard, 143-161 Nathan Road, Tsimshatsui, ph 2739 3888.

New Territories

CRC Department Store Ltd, 1/F-3/F, Nan Fung Centre, 258 Castle Peak Road, Tsuen Wan, ph 2498 3363.

Railway Duty Free, Departure Hall, KCR Lo Wu Terminal Building, Lo Wu, ph 2492 3844.

Yaohan Department Store (HK) Ltd, New Town Plaza, 18 Shatin Centre Road, Shatin, ph 2697 9338; Tuen Mun Town Plaza 209, Tuen Mun, ph 2450 3338.

Markets

Often you can pick up a really good bargain at the markets, but choose carefully as you definitely can't return anything, and if you are buying clothing, check all the seams and facings for faulty workmanship.

Cat Street is in the centre of Central's antiques quarter, off Hollywood Road, and is a flea market with inexpensive trinkets and bric-a-brac.

Li Yuen Street East and *Li Yuen Street West* are in Central, a short walk from the MTR station, and have stalls offering dress fabrics, clothes, scarves, sweaters, children's wear, cosmetics, etc. The stalls are generally open 10am-7pm.

Wanchai has a number of street markets. The Wanchai Road/Spring Garden Lane area has locally made designer jeans, children's wear and a variety of other goods. Queen's Road East is good for rattan and rosewood furniture.

Jardine's Bazaar, in the centre of Causeway Bay, has ladies' and children's wear, cosmetics and accessories. Further down the street are flower stalls and herbalists. The best time to shop here is between 11am and 6.30pm.

Stanley Market, on the south side of Hong Kong Island, is probably the best known of all the markets, and has a good selection of sports and casual wear, including good-quality silk and leather garments, and linen tableware. This market is generally open 10am-7pm.

Tung Choi Street in Mong Kok, is open daily 1-11pm, and is often known as the Ladies' Market, as it specialises in ladies' fashions, jewellery and accessories.

Temple Street, in the Yaumatei District of Kowloon, and *Poor Man's Nightclub* in front of the Macau Ferry Terminal on Hong Kong Island, are night markets that open when the sun goes down but are busiest between 8pm and 11pm. Unfortunately, they are not very well lit, which makes it hard to thoroughly check an article for faults, or to match colours. For more information on Temple Street, see the HKTA's *Yau Ma Tei Walking Tour*, available from HKTA Information and Gift Centres for HK$30.

Jade Market, under the flyover near Kansu Street in Yau Ma Tei, has all varieties of jade for sale ranging from the very cheap to top of the range. Buying jade is quite a dicey business, as it is difficult for anyone but an expert to pick the good from the bad. I really feel that it is better to buy your jade from a reputable dealer, or take an expert with you to the Jade Market.

This market is also included in the HKTA's Yau Ma Tei Walking Tour, and is open 10am-4pm.

Factory Outlets

The HKTA has a brochure entitled *Factory Outlets* which lists them all, with their phone numbers and opening hours. Goods available are ready-to-wear clothing, which are mostly export market seconds and so in Western sizes, and jewellery. Frequent visitors to Hong Kong often head straight for the factories rather than the shops, but whether you save much money is debatable. For one thing, you never know what is going to be on sale until you get there. One visit to a factory might be on the day when there is a large stock of women's casual gear going for next to nothing, but the return visit may be on men's throw-out day, with little to choose from in women's wear. Still, if you have the time it is worth picking up the brochure and seeing for yourself. Many of these factories only accept cash for transactions.

In the case of jewellery, credit cards are widely accepted.

Many of the outlets offer custom made jewellery, full guarantee certificates, jewellery repair and cleaning, and factory tours and inspections. Some also provide free transportation to their factories, or refund of taxi fares.

Tours

Many full-day and half-day tours are available, and there are many travel agents waiting to make your bookings. Your hotel desk usually has plenty of pamphlets and information on tours, and can make bookings for you. The HKTA also operates tours, and arrangements for these can be made at any HKTA Information and Gift Centre, ph 2807 6390 during the week, ph 2807 6177 weekends.

Following are some examples, with prices in HK$. Please treat these prices as a guide only, because it is impossible to predict fluctuations in prices (although it is a sure bet that they won't go down!).

Half-Day Tours

Hong Kong Island Tour - 4 hours, daily morning and afternoon departures - HK$220-290 adult, HK$110-210 child.

The routes for this tour vary from company to company but usually include: Victoria Peak; Aw Boon Haw (Tiger Balm) Gardens or Stanley Market; Repulse Bay and Deep Water Bay; Aberdeen Typhoon Shelter.

Ocean Park Tour: 4-6 hours, daily morning departure - HK$345-360 adult, HK$120-250 child.

Attractions include: Kids' world, Discovery of the Ancient World, Dinosaur discovery trail, the scenic cable car and the longest covered escalator in the world; Wave Cove; Ocean Theatre; Atoll Reef; and fun rides.

Middle Kingdom - is next door to Ocean Park - you may wish to give the tour a miss and just go to the Middle Kingdom yourself, will take about 4 hours price for entry is HK$140 adult, HK$70 child. Tour through 5000 years of Chinese history.

Kowloon and New Territories Tour - 4-5 hours, daily morning and afternoon departures - HK$120-150 adult, HK$70-110 child.

Travels through the urban and industrial areas of Kowloon and the scenic rural areas of the new Territories, including the

Kwai Chung Container Terminal and Tsuen Wan; a beach at Castle Peak; a stop at Lok Ma Chau (border); Tai Po; Shatin; and Amah Rock.

Historic Hong Kong Tour - 5 hours, Monday, Wednesday, Friday mornings - HK$295 adult, $245 child.
Visit Nam Pak Hong then to Possession Street, Statue Square, Noon Day Gun, Kowloon Walled city.

Heritage Tour - 5 hours, Monday, Wednesday, Friday and Saturday morning departure (except public holidays) - HK$325. Tour includes Lei Cheng Uk Han tomb and museum; Sam Tung Uk folk museum; Tai Fu Tai, a stately home; and Man Shek Tong ancestral hall.

Come Horseracing Tour - 5 hours, usually Saturday afternoon and Wednesday evening, September to June - HK$530. This tour is available to visitors over 18-years-old who arrived in HK less than 21 days before race day. Tour price includes entry to the Members' Enclosure, transfers, guide service, lunch/dinner at Royal Hong Kong Jockey Club, and racing guide. This tour visits meetings at either Happy Valley or Shatin.

Sung Dynasty Village Tour - Tour A: daily 10.30am-1pm - HK$250 adult, HK$170 child. Tour B: Mon-Fri noon-3.30pm - HK$250 adult, HK$170 child. Tour C: Mon-Fri 3-6pm - HK$190 adult, HK$150 child. Tour D: daily 5.30-8.30pm - HK$250 adult, HK$170 child. Complete tour of the replica of a city from the Sung Dynasty, including a Chinese meal or snack.

Open Top Tram Tour - 2 hours, daily morning and afternoon departures - HK$180 adult, HK$140 child. An open-top bus ride from Central to the tram depot, followed by an antique tram tour past Western District, Central, Wanchai and Causeway Bay. Unlimited soft drinks are served on the tram.

Factory Outlets Shopping Tour - 4 hours, Mon, Wed and Sat morning departures - HK$50 adult, HK$30 child. Visits a jewellery factory, a Chinese arts and crafts store and duty free shops.

Half-Day Cruises

One Hour Harbour Tour - daily morning and afternoon departures - HK$180 adult, HK$140 child.

Cruise around Victoria Harbour passing Western Anchorage, Macau Ferry Wharf, Central Commercial District, Wanchai, Causeway Bay Typhoon Shelter, North Point and Tsimshatsui East. Unlimited soft drinks included in the price. Highlight of the morning tour is the firing of the Noon Day Gun.

Cheung Chau Island Tour - Tour A: 4 hours Mon-Sat, morning departure - HK$165 adult, HK$105 child. Tour B: 7 hours Mon-Fri, morning departure - HK$300 adult, HK$250 child.

Cruise through Victoria Harbour past small islands of the South China Sea to tour Cheung Chau Island. For Tour B, a Chinese or European set lunch is served at the Warwick Hotel, and extra time is allowed for exploring or for a swim.

Harbour Tour - 2 hours, daily morning and afternoon departure - HK$200 adult, HK$110 child.

Cruise around Victoria Harbour, passing Ocean Terminal, Yau Ma Tei Typhoon Shelter, Western District, Central, Wanchai, Causeway Bay, North Point, Lantau Island suspension bridge and back to Tsimshatsui. Free soft drinks.

Aberdeen Lunch Cruise - 4 hours, daily morning departure - HK$360 adult, HK$260 child.

Cruise around Victoria Harbour, the Typhoon Shelter, Western Anchorage and some of Hong Kong's western islands to Aberdeen; return through Sulphur Channel, past Kennedy Town to Central. Includes a Dim Sum lunch aboard a floating restaurant in Aberdeen.

Aberdeen Sampan Tour - 20 minutes, daily from 9am-5pm - HK$40 adult, HK$30 child. Cruise around Aberdeen Typhoon Shelter on board a licensed and insured Chinese sampan. Guide and commentary are included.

Wan Fu Cruises - 2-4 hours - HK$250-435 adult, HK$205-325 child. Cruises usually include Victoria Harbour, with most going to Aberdeen, Clearwater Bay or Repulse Bay. One goes to

Cheung Chau Island. Unlimited drinks and snack or lunch are served on board.

Duk Ling Cruises - 1.5 hours, morning and afternoon departures - HK$150 per person. Unlimited drinks are served throughout a junk cruise around Victoria Harbour.

Whole Day Tours

The Land Between - 6 hours, Mon-Sat morning departure - HK$385 adult, HK$335 child. Travel through Kowloon to the rural New Territories, and up Hong Kong's highest mountain, Tai Mo Shan. Stops: a Buddhist temple, Luen Wo Market, a bird sanctuary at Luk Kent, Sam Mun Tsai fishing village and Tai Po. A Chinese lunch at a restaurant in the New Territories is followed by the return trip to Kowloon via Shatin racecourse and the Lion Rock Tunnel.

Sports and Recreation Tour - 8 hours, Tuesday and Friday morning departure - HK$430 includes lunch and admission, but excludes hiring charges of sports facilities. No child fare.

Visits the Clearwater Bay Golf and Country Club (HK$1,000 per person, $300 for clubs abd $150 for golf cart) on Sai Kung Peninsula for golf, tennis, badminton, squash, table tennis or swimming. Bring appropriate sporting apparel.

Hong Kong Island Tour with Lunch - 6 hours, daily morning departure - HK$380 adult, HK$310 child. Includes a ride on the Peak Tram to Victoria Peak, Western District, and Wah Fu Estate. After a dim sum lunch at a floating restaurant in Aberdeen Typhoon Shelter, visit a jewellery factory and Stanley Market.

Ocean Park/Middle Kingdom Tour - 9 hours, daily departures - HK$495 adult, HK$280 child. Chinese lunch is included in this tour which visits both these sightseeing musts.

Whole Day Cruises

Lantau Island Monastery Tour - Tour A: with vegi-lunch, 7.5hours, Mon-Sat - HK$480 adult, HK$400 child. Tour B: 6.5 hours, Mon-Sat afternoon departure - HK$420 adult, HK$360 child. Cruise to Lantau, then coach to Cheung Sha Beach, passing Shek Pik Reservoir, to Tai O fishing village and Po Lin

Monastery. A vegetarian lunch is served at the Monastery on Tour A. Tour B includes a snack at a local restaurant.

Harbour Junk and Sung Dynasty Village Tour - 7.5 hours, Mon-Fri morning departure - HK$385 adult, HK$295 child. Cruise around Victoria Harbour and Yau Ma Tei Typhoon Shelter, then travel by coach to Sung Dynasty Village for a Chinese lunch and cultural performances.

Evening Tours
City-Harbour by Night - 5 hours, nightly - HK$680 adult, HK$540 child. A harbour cruise with unlimited drinks on board followed by a night view from the scenic mid-levels of Victoria Peak precedes a western dinner at the Revolving 66 Restaurant. The tour continues with a visit to the nightlife area of Lan Kwai Fong.

Tram Tour/Dinner Cruise/La Ronda Restaurant/Pearl of Hong Kong - 4.5 hours, nightly. **Dinner Cruise:** HK$390 adult, HK$335 child. La Ronda Restaurant: HK$510 adult, HK$480 child. *Pearl of Hong Kong:* HK$370 adult, HK$315 child. A tram ride through Western District and Central and on to Wanchai and Causeway Bay, with unlimited free drinks on board. Then a coach trip to the Poor Man's Nightclub night market, followed by a Chinese dinner on a cruise, a dinner at La Ronda Revolving Restaurant, or a buffet aboard the *Pearl of Hong Kong.*

Harbour Night Cruise - 1.5 hours, nightly - HK$250 adult, HK$160 child. A sunset cruise along the west coast of Hong Kong Island to Aberdeen and back to Central with unlimited free drinks on board.

Open Top Bus Tour with Buffet Dinner Cruise - 5 hours, nightly - HK$550 adult, HK$380 child. Bus tour from Tsimshatsui, passing Yau Ma Tei Typhoon Shelter, Lung Cheung Road Lookout, resettlement estates, and Nathan Road's Golden Mile, followed by a western style buffet dinner aboard a cruising restaurant.

Sunset Cruise - 4 hours, nightly - HK$250 adult, HK$150 child;

or with dinner - HK$390 adult, HK$310 child.

A cruise through Yau Ma Tei Typhoon Shelter, then to Aberdeen for a one-hour stop with optional Chinese dinner at one of the famous floating restaurants. Free drinks are served on cruise.

Kowloon By Night and Buffet Dinner Cruise - 5 hours, nightly - HK$365 adult, HK$300 child.

Tour begins with a pre-dinner cocktail at a bar, followed by a visit to the Temple Street night market. A buffet dinner is served on a boat with live music and dancing.

Cultural Diversions - 3 hours, Monday and Thursday - HK$320 adult, HK$270 child. Children under six years not admitted.

A guided tour of the Hong Kong Cultural Centre's facilities is followed by two cultural performances and a Chinese banquet at the Centre's Cantonese restaurant, overlooking the night scene of Victoria Harbour.

Tours to China

Day trips to Shenzhen are easy to arrange from Hong Kong, and cost around HK$660-720. Any travel agent can do this, but it takes about 48 hours to get everything organised and obtain the necessary visa for China. The trip, by coach or train, takes in a visit to a commune, lunch and drive around the countryside of Shenzhen county, with stops at reservoirs, arts and crafts shops,some theme parks such as Splendid China etc.

Day trips to Zhongshan can be made from Macau. These involve an early start because it is necessary to travel to Macau by jetfoil, but the tour includes the home village of Dr Sun Yat-sen, the man who helped to found modern China - HK$880-895.

Shekou/Guangzhou trips begin with a hovercraft ride to Shekou to visit the exhibition of the Terracotta Warriors, a kindergarten and a free market. Then you travel by coach to Guangzhou, with lunch on the way, to visit the zoo, the Dr Sun Yat-sen Memorial Hall, Yuexiu Park or Guangzhou Museum - HK$1,200.

Side trips into China are available in conjunction with your trip to Hong Kong. These can be up to 4 days/3 nights, and there are several choices of itinerary, with some including a visit to Beijing. Side-trips can be booked in Hong Kong but you must have a Visa which is best obtained before you leave for Hong Kong as it takes more than several days to organise this once you are there.

Tours to Macau
One and two day packages to Macau can also be arranged when booking a Hong Kong Holiday, and these are good if time is of the essence. They only give a taste of Macau, though, and the Portuguese colony deserves much more. Read the chapter on Macau to whet your appetite.

The view from Victoria Peak

Aberdeen

The gates to Macau

Sport

Hong Kong is the venue for many international sporting events, including the annual Rugby Sevens, the Hong Kong Open Golf Championship, the Coast of China Marathon, the biennial China Sea Race, and the Dragon Boat Festival.

Horse Racing

Probably the most popular regular spectator sport is Horse Racing, and two tracks, Happy Valley on Hong Kong Island, and Shatin in the New Territories, have meetings on Wednesday nights, Saturday afternoons and sometimes on Sundays from September to June.

On-course betting is computerised, and off-course betting is available at outlets known as Off-course Betting Centres (OCBCs), which are easy to find. Apart from the local lottery, betting on the races is the only legal form of gambling in Hong Kong. Visitors over 18 years, who have been in Hong Kong less than 21 days can go to the races on the HKTA's *Come Horseracing Tour* (see Tours), or they can go independently as guests of the Hong Kong Jockey Club. On race day, go to the Badge Enquiry Office at the main entrance to the Members' Enclosure at either race course, and on presentation of your passport, and HK$50, you can buy a ticket allowing entry to the Members' Enclosure and the snack kiosk. Tickets are sold on a first-come-best-served basis.

Detailed form guides are published in the English-language newspapers, and betting is frantic and big at both courses. The record stands at HK$850 million in one day!

Martial Arts

If you happen to be up and moving around just after dawn (or, on the other hand, you may be just getting home after a night on the town), you will probably see devotees of martial arts performing mental and physical exercises, known as *tai chi chuan* (Chinese shadow-boxing) in parks and deserted streets.

Kowloon Park in Tsimshatsui, Chater Gardens in Central,

and Victoria Park in Causeway Bay, are among the best places to watch these routines.

For enquiries regarding martial arts, get in touch with the Hong Kong Chinese Martial Arts Association, ph 2394 4803.

Walking and Hiking

A number of leaflets on country parks and walks are available from Hong Kong Government Publications, G/F, GPO Building, Central, Hong Kong Island.

There are 21 Country Parks offering a range of facilities for walkers, and details of the parks and information on getting to them can be obtained from the Country Parks Authority, Agriculture and Fisheries Department, 12/F, 393 Canton Road, Kowloon, ph 2733 2132.

Tennis

Public courts are in short supply, and prices range from HK$40 per hour during the day to HK$75 per hour during the evening. Enquiries can be made at: Victoria Park, Causeway Bay, ph 2570 6186; Bowen Road, Wanchai, ph 2528 2983; the Tennis Centre, Wong Nai Chung Gap Road, ph 2574 9122; and Hong Kong Sports Institute in Shatin, New Territories, ph 2605 1212.

Squash

Most courts are found in private complexes or sports clubs, but there are public courts at Kowloon Tsai Park, ph 2336 7878; Li Chi Kok Indoor Games Sports Hall, Kowloon, ph 2745 2796; Queen Elizabeth Stadium, Victoria Park, ph 2570 6186; Hongkong Squash Centre, Cotton Tree Drive, Hong Kong Island, ph 2521 5072. Bookings must be made in person, and prices range from HK$20 to HK$40 per half hour.

Badminton and Table Tennis

Badminton is one of Hong Kong's most popular sports, with 64 participating clubs. Courts can be hired for about HK$43 per hour at several venues, including Queen Elizabeth Stadium, Wanchai, Hong Kong Island, ph 2557 6793. Table tennis can also be played at this stadium for about HK$30 per hour.

Swimming

Hong Kong is said to have more Olympic-size swimming pools per head of population than anywhere else in the world, but most of them are in private clubs. The urban Councils have public swimming complexes, which are cheap, and most hotels have their own pool.

The beaches are extremely crowded in summer.

Windsurfing

Sai Kung, Stanley and Cheung Chau are recommended for this sport. The Windsurfer Centre at Cheung Chau is next to the Warwick Hotel. Hire from Patrick, ph 2813 2372 for Stanley or Cheung Chau. Cost is $120 per hour.

Sailing

The Royal Hong Kong Yacht Club, at Kellett Island, Causeway Bay, ph 2832 5972, has reciprocal arrangements with many of the overseas clubs. Other yacht clubs include the Aberdeen Boat Club, the Aberdeen Marina Club, and the Hebe Haven Yacht Club. Companies that charter junks can be contacted through the HKTA.

Water Skiing

The Deep Water Bay Speedboat Co, ph 2812 0391, can arrange for you to hire a boat, driver and skis for around HK$390 per hour.

Diving

For information on diving clubs, contact the Sea Dragon Skin-Diving Club, ph 2891 2113.

Fishing

You have to have a licence to fish in Hong Kong's reservoirs, and this can be obtained from the Water Supplies Department, in Causeway Bay, ph 2890 0222. The season is from September to the end of March, and there are restrictions as to quantity and size of certain fish. Applicants for a fishing licence must be over 13-years-old.

Golf

For Visitors from countries such as Canada, USA, Australia and New Zealand and the UK golf is outrageously expensive. Visitors can play at the Royal Hong Kong Golf Club, home of the Hong Kong Open, for a green fee of around HK$1000 for 18 holes. It is also possible to hire clubs, buggies and caddies. The Club is at Fanling in the New Territories, ph 2670 1211.

The RHKGC also has a 9-hole course at Deep Water Bay on Hong Kong Island, and visitors can play there for about HK$400 on the weekends. No advance reservations can be made, so it is wise to be an early bird.

The Discovery Bay Golf Club, Lantau Island, ph 2987 7271, welcomes visitors on weekdays, and the green fee is HK$600.

Cycling

The most popular places for cycling are Shatin, Tai Wai and Tai Po in the New Territories, Shek O on Hong Kong Island, and Silvermine Bay on Lantau Islands. The price for hiring a bike is around HK$15, and they are available at many places in the rural areas, but you are advised to have someone write in Chinese what type of bike you require, as often people in these areas don't speak or understand English.

Horse Riding

Horses can be hired from Lantau Tea Gardens Ltd, ph 2985 8161, for HK$200 per half hour. Also from the Jockey Club stables in Pookfulam, ph 2550 1359.

Lawn Bowls

Public facilities are available at Victoria Park, Causeway Bay, and visitors can play on weekday afternoons or all day on weekends for HK$60 per hour. Bowls can be hired.

Ten-Pin Bowling

Bowling centres that can be easily reached by the MTR include: South China Bowling Centre, Causeway Bay, ph 2890 8528. With the South China Bowling Centre, visitors have to apply for temporary membership which costs HK$100. Cost per game per person is HK$23.00 after 5.00pm.

Roller Skating

Two venues for this sport are: Sportsworld Association, Telford Gardens, Kowloon, ph 2757 2211; and Rollerworld, Cityplaza, Hong Kong Island, ph 2567 0391.

Ice Skating

The ice rink at Lai Chi Kok Amusement Park, is open 9am-9.30pm daily, with four sessions. Cityplaza Phase II, Taikoo Shing, Hong Kong Island, ph 2567 0391, is open daily 7am-10pm, Wed, Thurs and Fri until 10.30pm.

Jogging

Probably the best place to jog is Bowen Road, which stretches from Stubbs Road to Magazine Gap Road on Hong Kong Island. It is closed to traffic for the most part, and has good views of the harbour. Also on Hong Kong Island, but less spectacular, is the jogging track at Victoria Park, Causeway Bay.

There is also traffic-free jogging along the waterfront promenade at Tsimshatsui East.

A Running Clinic is held on Hong Kong Island every Sunday morning at 7.30am. Telephone the Hong Kong Adventist Hospital, Mon-Fri mornings only, on 2574 6211.

Because of the high humidity and heat, it is wise to take plenty of water along when you go for a jog.

Sightseeing

The words 'Hong Kong' mean 'Fragrant Harbour', although 'fragrant' is not a word that immediately springs to mind when you first encounter Victoria Harbour. ('Breathtaking' is one word you might think of, but it has two meanings, doesn't it?) Nevertheless, the harbour was the reason for the beginnings of the settlement, and today is one of the busiest in the world. No trip to Hong Kong would be complete without a cruise of some kind, and a trip on the Star Ferry is probably the cheapest sightseeing tour you will find anywhere. The journey between Hong Kong Island and the Kowloon Peninsula only takes about eight minutes.

The skyscrapers of the Central District of Hong Kong Island seem to rise out of the water, and have actually been built on land reclaimed from the sea, with money generated from the world's third biggest financial centre, being surpassed only by London and New York. Hong Kong is also the world's largest exporter of watches, toys and clothes.

The fact that Hong Kong is small as tourist destinations go, means that sightseeing does not require any long-distance trips. Everything is close and handy, except, of course, for the 235 outlying islands, but you will only be interested in one or two of those.

Hong Kong Island

The Island's Central District is the business hub of the territory, with high-rise office blocks, banks and up-market shops. To the east of Central is Wanchai, once the haunt of sailors, bars and good-time girls. It still has a few bars and nightclubs, but they are being overtaken by office blocks. Beyond Wanchai is Causeway Bay, home to hotels, restaurants, department stores and dozens of small shops. The southern side of the island is largely residential, with apartment blocks and leisure facilities.

Here is found industrial Aberdeen, and, further east, Repulse Bay and Stanley, known for their beaches and views.

North Shore

Central District
(Map pages 78-79)

How To Get There
From Kowloon, by ferry, tunnel bus or MTR.
From other parts of Hong Kong Island by MTR's Island line, trams and buses.

Attractions
City Hall is situated to the east of the Star Ferry concourse, and consists of two blocks. The High Block contains, on the 10th and 11th floor, galleries with changing exhibitions of Chinese ceramics and bronzes, and cultural artifacts. The Low Block has a concert hall and theatre.

Adjacent to City Hall is the pick-up point for a free shuttle bus to the lower terminus of the Peak Tram in Garden Road.

Statue Square, on Chater Road, has a statue of Sir Thomas Jackson, an early Chief Manager of the HongkongBank. On the opposite side of Chater Road is the *Cenotaph*, which commemorates Hong Kong's war dead. This area can be reached by a pedestrian underpass running under Connaught Road from the Star Ferry pier.

There are several buildings in this vicinity that bear the names of the territory's earliest adventurers.

The Legislative Council is to the east of Statue Square. Formerly the supreme court, the building has granite pillars and a pediment carving of Blind Justice typical of late-Victorian colonial architecture, but the tiled Chinese-style roof seems a little out of character.

The HongkongBank building in Queens Road Central is said to be the world's most costly building of its type, and attracts architectural students from all over. The first phase was completed in June, 1985, and the highest level of *fung shui* expertise was needed to advise on the new position for the bronze lions who have guarded the bank since 1935.

St John's Cathedral, on Garden Road, was consecrated in 1849, and is believed to be the oldest Anglican church in the Far East. Within the Cathedral complex is a red-brick building with green shutters which was originally a French Mission. A booklet on the history of the Cathedral is available at the nearby Old Hall.

From the entrance to the HongkongBank, walk up the stone steps on the other side of the road to Battery Path.

Victoria Barracks has recently been redeveloped, and is the territory's largest pleasure ground, with fountains, waterfalls, lakes, greenhouses, and a 3000sqm walk-through aviary housing melanesian birds.

The *Museum of Tea Ware*, is located within the Barracks, in Hong Kong's oldest surviving colonial-style building, Flagstaff House. The museum has displays of porcelain, earthen-ware, gold teapots, bowls, trays, ewers and water pots. The collection was started by Dr K.S. Loo, who donated the pieces for public display. Flagstaff house was completed in 1846, and was the home of the Commander-in-Chief of the British Forces. The museum is open daily, except Wed, 10am-5pm, and there is no admission charge. From near the Peak Tram Terminus, walk along the pedestrian subway that goes under Cotton Tree Drive, leading to a pathway where directions to the Museum are posted.

The Zoological and Botanical Gardens has its main entrance in Upper Albert Road, about a 10 minute walk up the hill from the Hilton Hotel. Or you can take Bus 3 or 12 from City Hall and get out at the Caritas Centre and follow the uphill path.

The Gardens were established in 1864, in the traditional Victorian manner, complete with wrought-iron bandstand. The

Zoo was added in 1975 and has quite a few animals, but the main attractions are the aviaries which have a splendid assortment of exotic birds. In fact the Gardens have had great success in breeding birds that were almost extinct, and they supply many zoos around the world.

Government House is near the Gardens, and was built in 1855, with restoration work being carried out by the Japanese during their World War II occupation of Hong Kong. The grounds are known for their azaleas and rhododendrons. One Sunday every year (usually in March) the public is admitted.

Central Police Station on Hollywood Road, forms one of Hong Kong's biggest clusters of Victorian buildings, some dating back to the early years of the colony.

Lan Kwai Fong is an L-shaped cobblestoned lane that is home to numerous restaurants. It is a very 'in' place with young locals.

The Police Station and Lan Kwai Fong are a 10 minute walk up the hill from the Pedder Street exit of Central MTR station.
The area around *Li Yuen Streets East and West*, *Pottinger Street* and *Wing On Street* has many upmarket shopping malls, street markets, and alleys crammed with bargain clothing, costume jewellery and fabrics.

The Peak

A trip to the top of Victoria Peak should be compulsory for all visitors to Hong Kong, for it affords a 360 degree view of almost the whole territory. On a clear day, you can see, maybe not forever, but certainly the mountains of the New Territories and the many islands of the South China Sea. It is really is one of the most incredible views in the world.

How To Get There

A free shuttle bus runs between the Star Ferry/City Hall and the lower terminus of the Peak Tram on Garden Road. The tram takes you to the Peak Tower area, and from there you can walk, or take a taxi, to the gardens at the summit of the Peak.

Alternatively, the no 1 Peak minibus leaves from HMS Tamar, near City Hall, and the no 15 double-decker bus leaves from the Central Bus Station, Exchange Square. Both terminate at the Peak Tower.

Attractions

The Peak Tram is the first attraction. In the 19th century, it took about three hours and a succession of coolie-operated sedan chairs to reach the Peak. Then, in 1888, the Peak Tram commenced operation and the journey was reduced to eight minutes. In 1989, the system was modernised, making it one of the most advanced in the world.

The tram operates 7am-midnight, with services every 10 minutes, and climbs almost vertically to the Peak Tower. It amazes me that in its entire history there has never been an accident, nor has anyone tried to bail out when the up-going got tough.

The Peak Tower is an elliptical structure at the upper terminus of the Peak Tram, and has a coffee shop, a restaurant, a post office, supermarket, various souvenir shops, and a viewing deck.
Harlech Road and *Lugard Road* offer a flat, circular hour-long hike around the Peak, with panoramic views, and the walk begins to the right of the exit from the Peak Tower.

Mount Austin Road, opposite the Tram terminus exit, takes the energetic up to the summit of the peak, via the *Victoria Peak Gardens*, all that remain of the Governor's summer residence, Mountain Lodge. The Lodge was a seven-bedroom Victorian grange, built in 1900 at a cost of HK$97,000, but it was never particularly patronised because most of the time it was shrouded in mist. By 1934, the Governor had organised a new retreat in Fanling, and Mountain Lodge was allowed to fall into disrepair. It was finally demolished in 1946.

Today, the gardens are tended by the Urban Council, and provide a popular weekend spot for many local residents.

Pok Fu Lam Country Park has its upper entrance on Pok Fu Lam Reservoir Road, to the left of the Peak Tower exit, on the other side of the road. There is a bar across the entrance, but only to restrict vehicles, people are free to wander in. The park has spectacular views at its higher levels, and is the most accessible of Hong Kong's country parks.

Western District

How To Get There
By taxi or on foot from Star Ferry, or by MTR to Sheung Wan station, or by tram. From Central District, take bus no 26 from in front of HongkongBank head office to Hollywood Road.

Attractions
Western Market, on the corner of Connaught Road and Morrison Street, is a beautifully reconstructed Edwardian building reminiscent of London's Covent Garden market. It originally opened in 1858 as one of the first produce markets, and reopened in late 1991, but now its shops sell specialty gifts and souvenirs. The market is also home to a food centre that offers traditional cuisine. The shops are open daily 10am-7pm, the restaurant 11am-11.30pm.

Hollywood Road is well-known for its antique and curio shops, and at its western end is *Possession Street*, where there is a plaque marking the spot where British naval officers first came ashore and hoisted the Union Jack (and probably gave three cheers) on January 26, 1841.

Man Mo Temple, on the corner of Hollywood Road and Ladder Street, is named for its two principal deities - Man, the god of literature, and Mo, the god of war. The present building dates from the early years of British rule, and the interior is noted for its many incense burners, some of which hang in immense spirals from the ceiling, and heavily carved wooden chairs. It is possible to have your fortune told in the temple. Incidentally, Ladder Street gets its name from the steeply rising stone staircase, up which the wealthy were carried in sedan chairs.

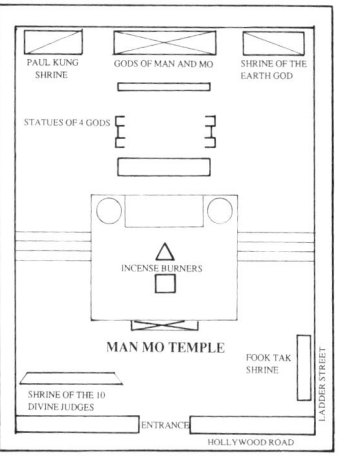

Lascar Row or *'Cat Street'* was once famous as a hangout for all types of baddies, but it is now an improvised flea market. The Cat Street Galleries are in nearby Lok Ku Road, and are devoted to fine arts, handmade works of art and antiques. The lions guarding the entrance to the Gallery are a full-sized reproduction of the Nine Dragon Monument in Behai Park in Beijing.

Bonham Strand is known for its snake shops. Snake is a seasonal delicacy, often served in soups, and is reputed to combat winter chills. It is also served in various ways to combat rheumatism.

Man Wah Lane, which runs off Bonham Strand, has several shops that make and sell 'chops'. Chops, or seals, are made of soapstone, carved in various shapes and sizes. On the bottom end is engraved the name of the owner, and the chops were used as signatures for transactions. Some elderly Chinese still prefer to use a chop rather than sign their name. Experts can read the various chops stamped down the side of ancient Chinese paintings and wall hangings, and can say who had owned them over the years.

The chops make good souvenirs, and take about an hour to engrave with an appropriate translation of your name. They come in an elegant little box, complete with a vermilion ink pad. Prices vary according to the amount of carving on the block, and to the amount of characters in your name. Popular carvings are the signs of the Chinese zodiac.

Wing Sing Street also runs off Bonham Strand, further to the east, and is better known as Egg Street. Here, hundreds of eggs of all types and sizes are sold, and while you may not be in the market for an egg, it is fascinating to watch the people unpacking eggs from China and 'candling' them in front of naked light bulbs to test for freshness. The chanting that accompanies this is an ancient form of counting.

Wanchai
(see map overleaf)
The eastern end of Hong Kong Island's northern shore has changed faster than any other part of the territory. Reclamation schemes have filled in sections of the harbour, creating new

land for multi-storey housing estates and public buildings. Along with these have come shopping malls, restaurants, bars, and exhibition and concert halls.

How To Get There
From Kowloon, there is a ferry direct to Wanchai.
    The area is also accessible by tram and MTR.

Attractions
Academy for Performing Arts, often shortened to APA, the *Hong Kong Arts Centre* and the *Hong Kong Convention and Exhibition Centre* are situated near one another at the western end of Wanchai.

Queen's Road East was once the waterfront area of Wanchai, and is home to many fine blackwood cabinet makers, rattan furniture shops, and in the overhanging buildings, blind fortune tellers, on whom the Chinese place great reliance. Fortune tellers can also be found in the Tai Wong Temple, at no 129-131, and in the nearby shrine in Tik Lung Lane.

Hopewell Centre, in Queen's Road East, is locally known as the Stone Cigar, and was Hong Kong's tallest building before the new Bank of China Tower was completed. There is a revolving restaurant on the top floor, reached by a glass-walled lift that is outside the building. The ground floor entrance to the building is on Queen's Road East, but the carpark is 17 storeys higher(!), and accessed from Kennedy Road.

Spring Garden Lane and *Wanchai Road* are market areas with shops, stalls selling fruit, vegetables and locally made denim.

Wanchai Post Office, at the junction of Queen's Road East and Wanchai Gap Road, is the oldest post office in the colony and is a protected historic building. It's worth having a look inside.
Lover's Rock, on the hill behind Wanchai, is a 9m pointed rock sitting on a ledge about 30m from the street level. Legend has it that hundred of years ago a beautiful girl was abandoned by her lover, and went to see the local fortune-teller for advice. He told her to offer prayers to the rock, and sure enough, she got her man. The rock is locally known as Yan Yuen Shek, which can mean either Lovers' or Maiden's Rock, and the 6th, 16th

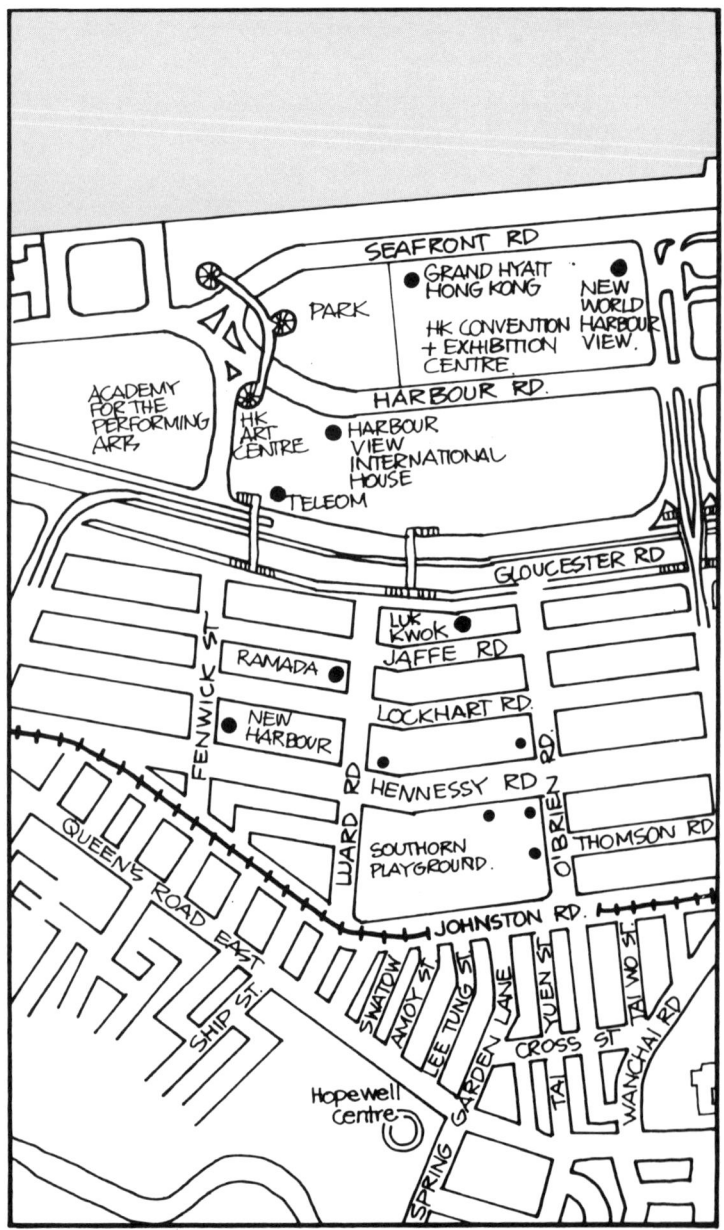

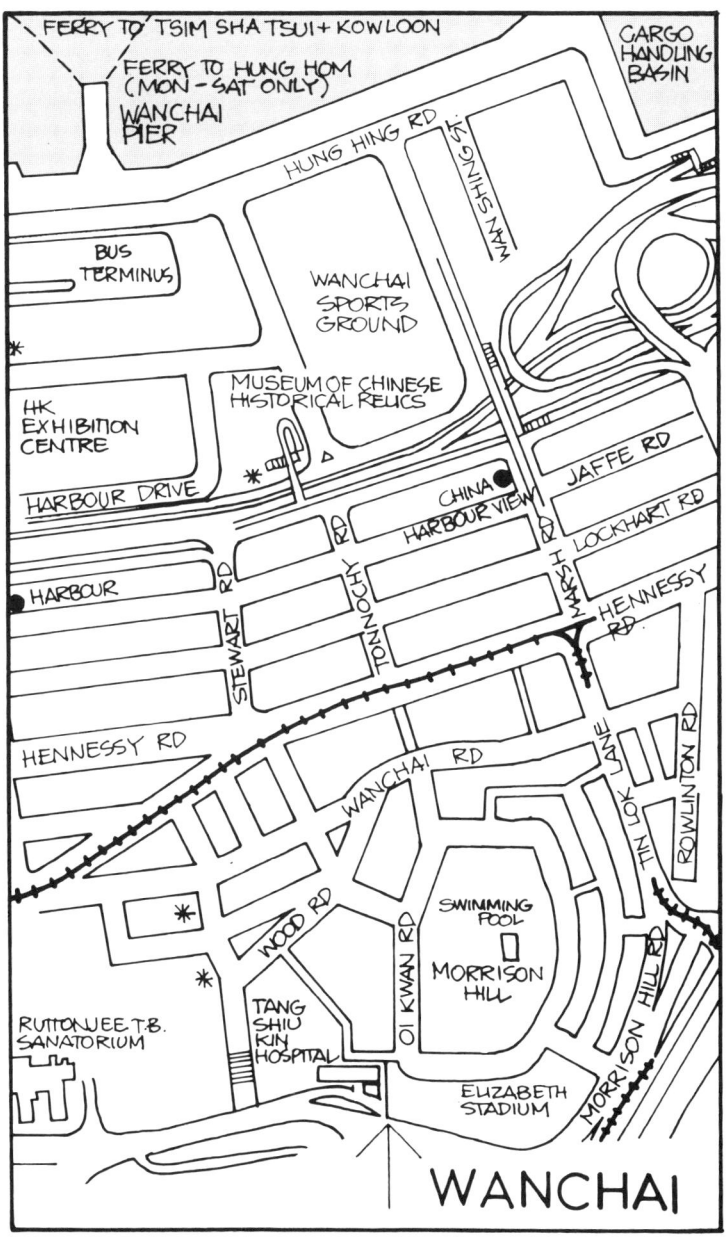

FERRY TO TSIM SHA TSUI + KOWLOON

FERRY TO HUNG HOM
(MON - SAT ONLY)
WANCHAI
PIER

CARGO
HANDLING
BASIN

HUNG HING RD

WAN SHING ST.

BUS
TERMINUS

WANCHAI
SPORTS
GROUND

MUSEUM OF CHINESE
HISTORICAL RELICS

HK
EXHIBITION
CENTRE

HARBOUR DRIVE

JAFFE RD

CHINA
HARBOUR VIEW

LOCKHART RD

STEWART RD

TONNOCHY RD

MARSH RD

HENNESSY RD.

HARBOUR

HENNESSY RD

WANCHAI RD

TIN LOK LANE

ROWLINTON RD

WOOD RD

OI KWAN RD

SWIMMING
POOL

MORRISON
HILL

MORRISON HILL RD

RUTTONJEE T.B.
SANATORIUM

TANG
SHIU
KIN
HOSPITAL

ELIZABETH
STADIUM

WANCHAI

and 26th days of the lunar months are the times that the rock is apparently most powerful. On these days, fortune tellers, soothsayers and incense sellers ply their trades along Bowen Road, cashing in on the legend and the lovelorn.

Happy Valley

How To Get There
By tram, or as part of HKTA tour.

Attractions
Situated between Wanchai and Causeway Bay, Happy Valley is the site of Hong Kong's oldest horse racing venue. The first races were held here in 1846 on land reclaimed from a disease-ridden swamp - a far cry from the facilities available today. For more information on the race meetings, see Sport and Recreation section.

Causeway Bay
(see map p114-115)
Situated between Wanchai to the west and North Point to the east, Causeway Bay is a shopping and entertainment district. There are Japanese department stores, street markets, temples and a typhoon shelter.

How To Get There
By MTR to Causeway Bay station, or by tram from Central. There are also plenty of buses and minibuses.

Attractions
The Noon-Day Gun is situated in a small garden opposite the Excelsior Hotel in Gloucester Road, and is still fired every day on the stroke of noon. It was immortalised by the late Noel Coward in his *Mad Dogs and Englishmen* song, which along with saying that these creatures "go out in the noon-day sun" also said, "In Hong Kong they strike a gong and fire off the noon-day gun". Originally, the firing of the gun was a penalty imposed on the Jardines trading company during the 19th century. The company had always welcomed its senior officers with a double-gun salute, then a senior naval officer took offence, saying that gun salutes were only allowed for officers

of flag rank. Accordingly, Jardines were ordered to fire a gun every day at noon, supposedly for ever, as a time signal for Hong Kong. The only other time the gun is ever fired is at midnight on New Year's Eve.

Food Street is between the Excelsior Hotel and the end of Gloucester Road, and is renowned for its many restaurants of every conceivable national cuisine.

Jardine's Bazaar and *Jardine's Crescent* are an open-air market area. The stalls in the Bazaar specialise in fashion items, although fairly down-market, and the Crescent has mostly old-fashioned shops selling dried food, medicinal herbs, and other traditional produce.

Victoria Park, bounded by Victoria Park Road, Gloucester Road, Causeway Road and Hing Fat Street, has Olympic-sized swimming pools, tennis courts, football fields, and other sporting facilities. In the early morning, the park attracts many devotees of traditional Chinese shadow boxing (*tai chi chuan*), which is worth watching if you happen to be in the vicinity at that time of day. A pedestrian bridge links the park with the typhoon shelter.

Causeway Bay Typhoon Shelter, and other shelters around the territory's coastline, are crammed with junks, sampans and other frail craft seeking safety, when a typhoon threatens, or during the Chinese New Year holidays. At other times, the waterfront is lined with boats, sometimes occupied by several generations of a family, together with their assortment of pet dogs and cats.

Tin Hau Temple, at the junction of Causeway Road and Tin Hau Temple Road, is situated on a granite platform high above the tram tracks. Before the reclaiming of so much land, this temple dedicated to the protector of those who make their living from the sea, was more appropriately on the waterfront.

Lin Fa Kung Street has a renovated octagonal-shaped temple that has some beautiful painted and carved decorations.

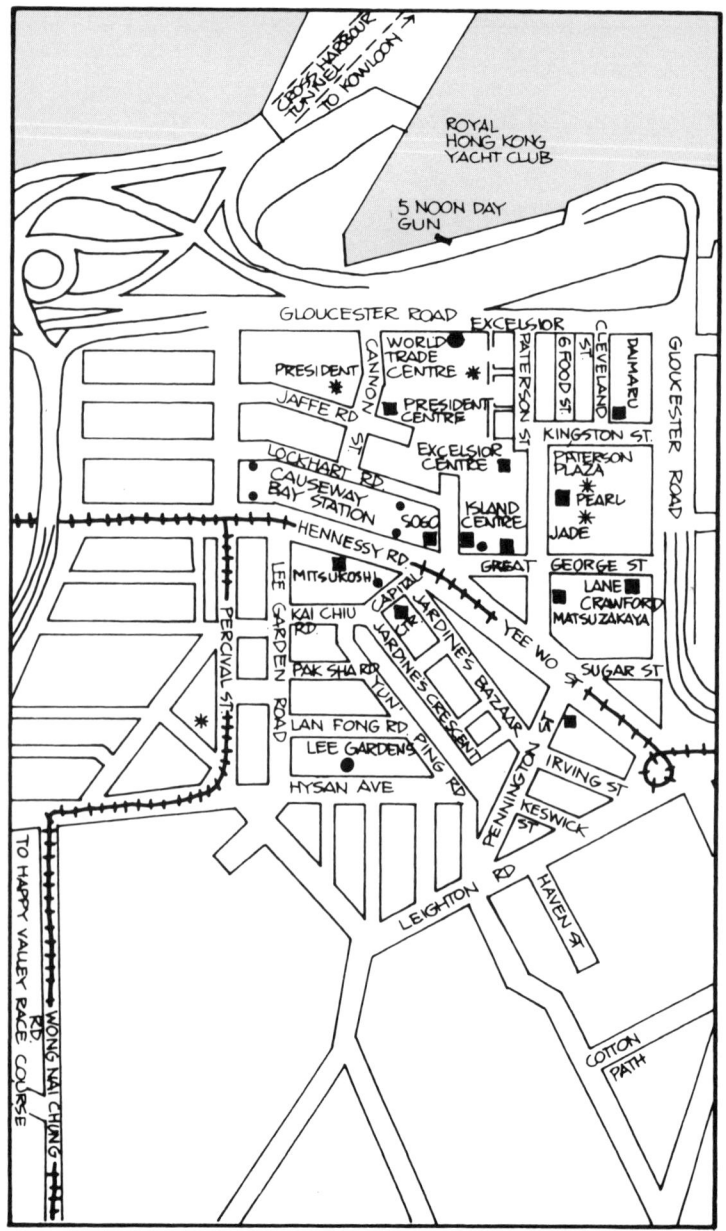

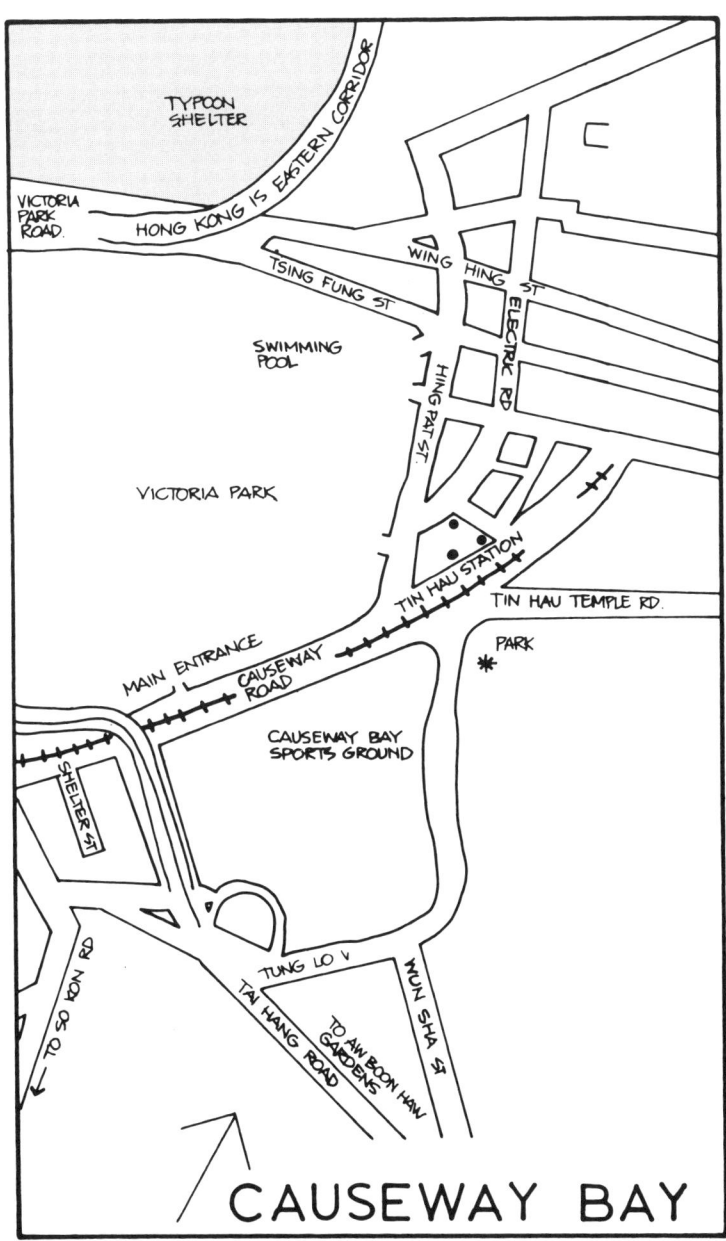

TYPOON SHELTER

VICTORIA PARK ROAD.

HONG KONG IS EASTERN CORRIDOR

WING HING ST

TSING FUNG ST

ELECTRIC RD.

SWIMMING POOL

HING PAT ST

VICTORIA PARK

TIN HAU STATION

TIN HAU TEMPLE RD.

MAIN ENTRANCE

CAUSEWAY ROAD

PARK

SHELTER ST

CAUSEWAY BAY SPORTS GROUND

TUNG LO V

WUN SHA ST

TO SO KON RD

TAI HANG ROAD

TO AW BOON HAW GARDENS

CAUSEWAY BAY

Aw Boon Haw Gardens are a short taxi ride from Causeway Bay off Tai Hang Road. Formerly known as the Tiger Balm Gardens, they were built in 1935 by local philanthropist, Aw Boon Haw, who also invented the famous Tiger Balm ointment, which supposedly cures everything but a broken heart.

The gardens are open daily 9.30am-4pm, and admission is free. They contain many plaster statues and scenes from Chinese mythology, usually showing in graphic detail the terrible things that may happen in the after life if we don't all behave ourselves. In a word, the gardens are tacky, but seem to gain something in photographs. Most people tend to go through at least one roll of film there.

South Side

While the north shoreline of Hong Kong Island has been altered considerably by land reclamation, the south side, except for Aberdeen, remains virtually unchanged. It still has sandy beaches, rocky inlets and country parkland, intermingled with upmarket residential complexes.

Aberdeen

Once a quiet fishing village, and the site of an incense factory which gave Hong Kong its name, Fragrant Harbour, Aberdeen is now a thriving town. Over the past decade, modern highrise housing, factory buildings and new roads have vastly altered its appearance.

How To Get There

From Central District, bus no 7 (HK$5, air-conditioned) or no 70 (HK$4.50 air-conditioned) from the Exchange Square bus terminal.

From Causeway Bay, bus no 72 (HK$4.50 air-conditioned) from Moreton Tce, or maxicab no 4 or 5 (HK$6) from Yun Ping Road.

Attractions

Aberdeen Harbour is best-known for its 'floating' population - people who live their lives on board moored boats, which are so close together that it is possible to walk from those furthest

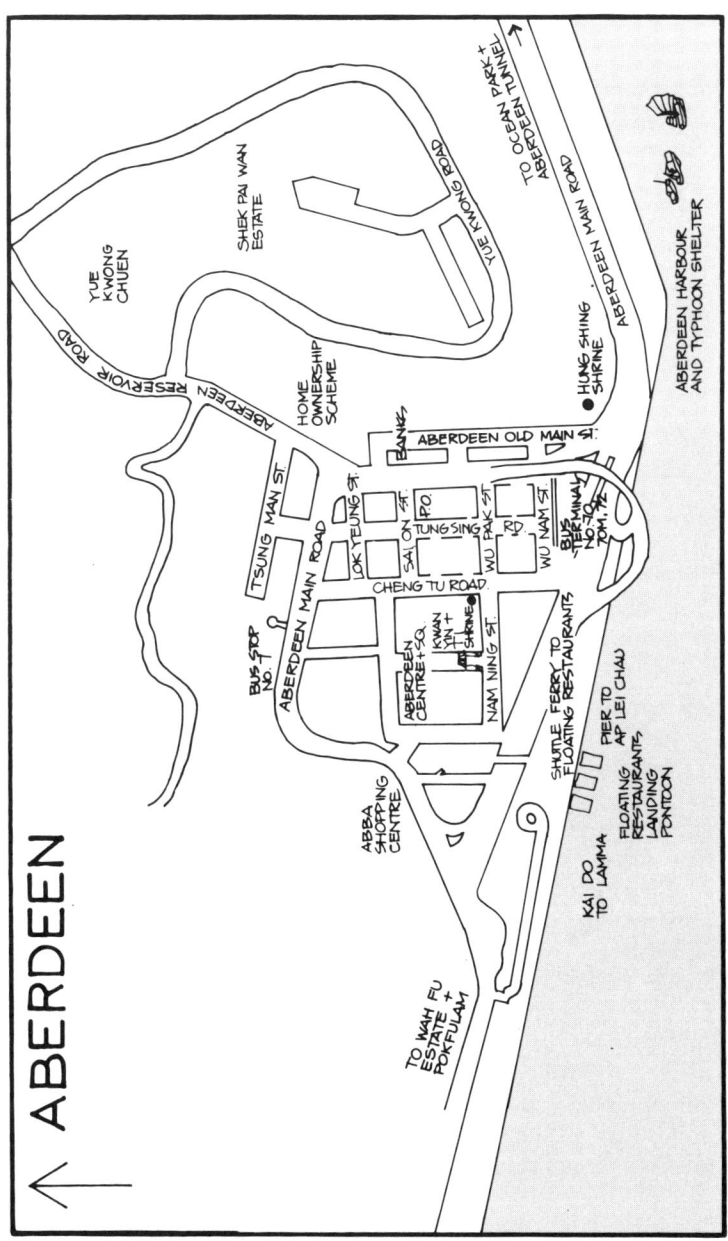

ABERDEEN

out over boat after boat to the shore. Although their numbers are declining due to increased low-cost housing on shore, it is worthwhile taking one of the guided sampan tours, which operate daily 9am-5pm from the main sea wall, opposite Aberdeen Centre. A 20 minute tour costs around HK$100 adult, HK$80 child.

The other attractions on the harbour are the two *floating restaurants*. They are elaborately decorated in the Chinese style, and when lit up at night must cause a terrible drain on the territory's electricity supply. They specialise in seafood, and are another must on any visitor's itinerary. Each restaurant has its own motor boats to ferry customers to and fro.

A good view of the harbour can be obtained from the centre of the bridge that links Aberdeen with Ap Lei Chau (Duck's Tongue Island).

Aberdeen Country Park is at the end of Aberdeen Reservoir Road, a short taxi ride from the town centre. The park has a visitor information centre, fitness trails, marked nature trails, and relics of World War II.

Ocean Park is South-east Asia's largest entertainment and leisure centre, and can be reached by cable car, or by the longest outdoor escalator in the world.

An Ocean Park Citybus leaves Admiralty MTR station, half-hourly from 9.30am, and the charge for transport and entrance is HK$163 adult, HK$84 child. The no. 6 minibus from Star Ferry, Hong Kong-side, travels to Ocean World Mon-Sat, except public holidays, and the fare is HK$5. Entrance to Ocean Park without transport costs is HK$140 adult, HK$70 child, which covers everything except food and drink, and the centre is open Mon-Sat 10am-6pm, Sun and public holidays 9am-6pm. For further information, ph 2552 0291.

Attractions include: a coral atoll, shows by dolphins, killer whales and divers; a glass-sided wave cove of seals and fairy penguins; an aviary; a butterfly house; fun-fair rides; and an adventure playground, dinosaur discovery trail, and film fantasia simulator.

Water World is adjacent to Ocean Park, and is run by the same people. It is a fun park with swimming pools, giant water slides, and a winding river. It is open daily (May to October) 10am-5pm, until 10pm at the height of summer. Admission is HK$65 adult, HK$33 child, which again includes all activities.

Middle Kingdom, near Ocean Park, is a 10,000sqm development where you can take a walk through the history of China. It consists of a series of full-size replicas of temples, shrines and street scenes, and public squares, pavilions, pagodas and palaces, which recreate the sights and sounds of China's thirteen dynasties. Tour guides lead visitors from one period to the next, beginning with the Xia Dynasty (2205BC) and finishing the trip with the completion of the Qing Dynasty in 1911AD, which is represented by a magnificent recreation of the Emperor's Summer Palace in Beijing.

At the end of the tour there is a theatre, modelled on the famous Empress Theatre in Beijing, where there are 45 minute shows of traditional Chinese performing arts - 3 shows Mon-Sat, 4 shows Sun and public holidays.

The complex also has a restaurant, snack bar, exhibition hall and gift shop, and is open daily, 10am-6pm. Admission is HK$140 adult, HK$70 child (6-7 years) for both Ocean Park and Middle Kingdom.

Beaches

The Island's gazetted beaches offer showers, changing facilities and toilets, cold drinks and snacks. Life savers are on duty during the summer, and the beaches get very crowded on the weekends and public holidays.

Shek O and the more distant *Big Wave Bay* are less accessible than most, which means that they are quite deserted during the week. *Deep Water Bay* is quite close to the road, and easily accessible by taxi from Central, but still has room to spare during the week.

Repulse Bay is a popular residential area, and is featured on many Hong Kong Island tour itineraries. The beach is also very popular, and so best to avoid on the weekends. It can be reached by bus no 6 or no 61 from Central Bus Station (Exchange Square).

The Chinese style building at the eastern end of the beach is the Life Guard Club, and the two huge statues are the gods

Kwun Yum and Tin Hau, both protectors of those who earn their living from the sea.

Repulse Bay also has a variety of shops and restaurants.

Stanley

A century ago Stanley was the haunt of pirates and smugglers, but today it is a residential area with about 6000 inhabitants. It is one of Hong Kong's oldest settlements.

How To Get There

From Central, buses no 6, 6A, 6X (HK$7.50) and no 260 (HK$10) from Exchange Square.

From Causeway Bay, bus no 63 (HK$5.50) from Tung Lo Wan Road (no service on Sun or public holidays), or bus no 65 (HK5.50) from Hennessy Road (Sun and public holidays only).

Attractions

Stanley Market is the best-known attraction, and is a mecca for visitors and locals looking for designer denim, mohair sweaters, silk and leatherware, hand-painted porcelain and souvenirs. It is always possible to pick up a real bargain at these markets.

The *Tin Hau Temple*, on the outskirts of Ma Hang Village, beyond the market, dates from 1767. Stanley was heavily bombed during World War II, and one which landed outside the temple, where the people had gathered to seek protection, did not explode. The credit for this, of course, was given to Tin Hau, the goddess of the sea, and the temple really comes alive at the time of the Tin Hau Festival in late April/early May.

One unusual item in the temple is a tiger skin, reportedly from an animal shot nearby during the Japanese Occupation.

Stanley has a colonial-style *police station*, which is a declared historical monument, and *wartime reminders* in the town are the cemetery, opposite St Stephen's Beach, and Stanley Prison, which was an internment camp from 1941 until mid-1945.

The major part of the peninsula is Stanley Fort, a British military installation which is off-limits to the general public.

Kowloon

On March 26, 1860, the tip of Kowloon Peninsula was ceded to Britain, and amounted to 12 sq km (5 sq miles), with six per cent of that taken up by Stonecutters Island, which was only for British military occupation. Boundary Street, a few blocks north of Mong Kok MTR station, marked the border with China until 1898, when 'new Kowloon' was formed from the leased New Territories.

Now, Kowloon is usually regarded as the area south of the range of hills which form Victoria Harbour's northern backdrop, and are the source, in legend anyway, of the Chinese name for the area, *Gow Lung*, which means 'Nine Dragons'.

According to Chinese mythology, every hill or mountain is home to a dragon, and when a Chinese emperor visited this part of the world, he counted the eight peaks north of the harbour and thought of bestowing the name 'Eight Dragons'. One of the emperor's courtiers, who definitely knew on which side his bread was buttered, carefully pointed out to his lord and master that as the emperor was the supreme dragon, everyone else present could see nine dragons. Hence the name, but it is not recorded what reward the courtier received.

The last century has seen Kowloon develop into a densely populated area, containing some of the territories most popular attractions.

Tsimshatsui

Tsimshatsui means 'sharp sandy point', and that is what it was in 1860, when only a few villagers shared the tip of land with the British troops. The promontory is now known as a major shopping and entertainment area, and for its official height restriction of the equivalent of 17 storeys, to ensure safe aircraft approaches to Hong Kong International Airport.

Attractions
The Clock Tower, alongside the Star Ferry Concourse, is 45m high and is all that remains of the original Kowloon-Canton

Railway Station, relocated to Hung Hom in 1975. The Tower is a good starting point for a walking tour of Tsimshatsui.

The Hong Kong Cultural Centre was built on the site of the old railway station and opened on November 5, 1989. The Centre includes a 2100-seat Concert Hall, 1750-seat Grand Theatre, a 300 to 500-seat Studio Theatre, six exhibition galleries for the Hong Kong Museum of Art collections, and restaurants, bars and other facilities. Its 'ski slope' roofline is a harbourside landmark that contrasts well with the domed design of the nearby Planetarium.

The Space Museum houses one of the most technically sophisticated planetariums in the world, which presents wide-screen Omnimax films and sky shows. One showing of each presentation is in English, and headphones for simultaneous translations, in English, Japanese, Mandarin and Cantonese, are available free of charge. Entrance to the Museum, including the Hall of Solar Sciences and the Exhibition Hall, is free, but admission to planetarium shows is HK\$30 adult, HK\$15 for students and the over 60s. Children under 6 years of age are not admitted. Open Wed-Mon, 2-9.30pm, and for show times, ph 2734 2722.

The Space Museum is within easy walking distance of the Kowloon Star Ferry concourse and Tsimshatsui MTR station.

Nathan Road is the best known street in Kowloon, and probably the widest in the territory. It begins at Salisbury Road and runs to the Boundary Road border, a distance of about 4km. The southern stretch is known as the Golden Mile, but originally the entire length was affectionately called Nathan's Folly. It was ordered to be built by Governor Matthew Nathan in the early 1900s, a time when there were very few inhabitants and consequently very little traffic. People laughed at what they thought was the unnecessary width of a street that virtually led to nowhere, but no-one's laughing today.

Kowloon Park is reached via an exit so marked from Tsimshatsui MTR station. It opened in 1989 and has an indoor heated Olympic-sized swimming pool complex and an air-conditioned games hall.

In the landscaped gardens there is a *Sculpture Walk* which features works by local crafts people, and at the northern end of the Walk is the major permanent exhibit, Sir Eduardo Paolozzi's bronze depiction of William Blake's *Concept of Newton*. The free sculpture exhibition is well lit at night, and is open every day.

Other outdoor attractions include a Chinese garden, bird lake, maze, lily pond, water and 'colour' gardens, banyan tree court, a children's playground, an aviary, and a roof garden. The park is open daily 6.30am-midnight, the Discovery Playground 6.30am-9pm, and the Aviary 6.30am-8pm.

Hong Kong Museum of History is temporarily housed in two converted barracks on the former site of the British Whitfield Barracks, within Kowloon Park. It has quite an extensive collection of archaeological specimens and historical photographs, and all captions are in English and Chinese. The museum is open Mon-Thurs and Sat 10am-6pm, Sun 1-6pm, and there is no admission fee.

The Jamia Masjid and Islamic Centre is also found in Kowloon Park, and was built in 1984, replacing a one-storey mosque built in 1896 for the Muslim Indian troops in the British army. Now there are approximately 50,000 Muslims in Hong Kong, and about half of them are Chinese. Guided tours of this traditionally styled mosque can be arranged by appointment, ph 2724 0095.

Harbour City, on Canton Road, is the territory's largest interconnected shopping mall, and incorporates Ocean Terminal, Ocean Centre and Ocean Galleries. It is also linked to other shopping centres on the other side of the road.

The oldest section is Ocean Terminal, opened in 1966 as a four-deck docking zone for international cruise liners. Liners still use these facilities, but the major mooring point is the China Ferry Terminal at the far end of Harbour City, next to the China Hong Kong City. It opened in 1988. Also included is Asia's first Planet Hollywood opened in 1994. Here besides Stallone and Schwarzenegger there is also a Bruce Lee room.

Tsimshatsui East - Hung Hom

Tsimshatsui East was built largely on reclaimed land and is bordered by Salisbury and Chatham Roads. It is mainly a hotel and shopping area.

How To Get There

From Tsimshatsui MTR station on the Tsuen Wan Line, by foot, or from Kowloon Star Ferry concourse, take minibus no 1 to Tsimshatsui East.

From Hong Kong Island, there is a direct hover ferry service daily from East Ferry Pier in Edinburgh Place, Central, to a pontoon landing opposite the Shangri-La Hotel. There is also a Star Ferry service from Central to Hung Hom.

Attractions

Hong Kong Science Museum on Science Museum Road, opened in April 1991. It has about 500 exhibits, the majority of which are of the "hands on" variety. The museum is open Tues-Fri 1-9pm, Sat-Sun and public holidays 10am-9pm, and admission is HK$25 adult, HK$15 student and child.

A *waterfront promenade* begins at the New World Centre and goes all the way to *Hung Hom*, and allows great views of the Harbour and Hong Kong Island.

Hung Hom is home to the *Hong Kong Coliseum*, *Hong Kong Polytechnic* and numerous factory outlets specialising in ready-to-wear fashions. The Coliseum, which opened in 1983, is a 12,500-seat pillar-less stadium for sporting events, exhibitions and concerts. It is built in the form of an upside-down pyramid.

Ko Shan Theatre has been renovated to seat 1000. It is part of a community arts centre located in Ko Shan Park and is a regular venue for Chinese Opera.

Yauma Tei

Situated north of Tsimshatsui and Jordan Road, Yau Ma Tei was once farmland, and in fact the name means 'place of sesame plants'. The HKTA have a guidebook entitled *Yau Ma Tei Walking Tour* which is available from their Information and Gift Centres for about HK$30.

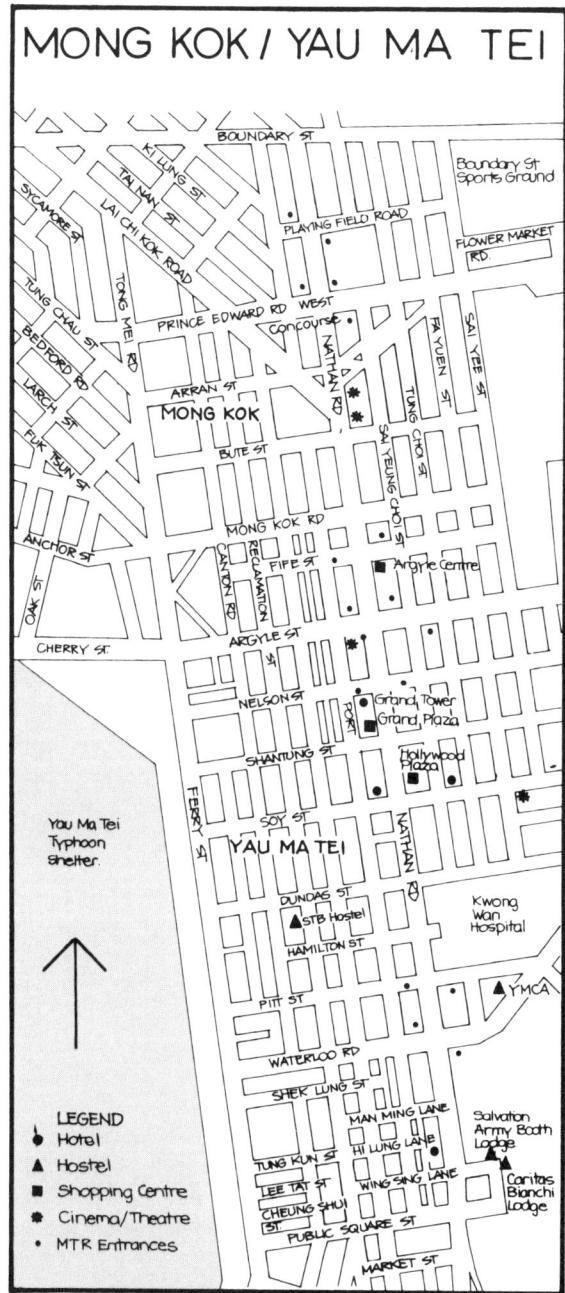

MONG KOK / YAU MA TEI

BOUNDARY ST

Boundary St Sports Ground

PLAYING FIELD ROAD

FLOWER MARKET RD.

K'I LUNG ST

TAI NAN ST

SYCAMORE ST

LAI CHI KOK ROAD

TONG MEI RD.

TUNG CHAU ST

BEDFORD RD

LARCH ST

FUK TSUN ST

PRINCE EDWARD RD WEST

Concourse

SAI YEE ST

NATHAN RD

FA YUEN ST

TUNG CHOI ST

SAI YEUNG CHOI ST

ARRAN ST

MONG KOK

BUTE ST

MONG KOK RD

ANCHOR ST

OAK ST

CANTON RD

RECLAMATION

FIFE ST

Argyle Centre

CHERRY ST.

ARGYLE ST

NELSON ST

Grand Tower
Grand Plaza

PORT

SHANTUNG ST

Hollywood Plaza

FERRY ST

SOY ST

NATHAN RD

Yau Ma Tei
Typhoon
Shelter.

YAU MA TEI

DUNDAS ST
STB Hostel

Kwong
Wan
Hospital

HAMILTON ST

PITT ST

YMCA

WATERLOO RD

SHEK LUNG ST

MAN MING LANE

Salvation
Army Booth
Lodge

TUNG KUN ST

HI LUNG LANE

LEE TAI ST

WING SING LANE

Caritas
Bianchi
Lodge

CHEUNG SHUI ST.

PUBLIC SQUARE ST

MARKET ST

LEGEND
● Hotel
▲ Hostel
■ Shopping Centre
✳ Cinema/Theatre
• MTR Entrances

How To Get There
There is a Tsuen Wan Line MTR Station in Yau Ma Tei, or keep walking along Nathan Road.

Attractions
Tin Hau Temple, in Public Square Street, is a terrace of five units, with the central, and largest being dedicated to Tin Hau, the goddess of fisherfolk. The other temples are to Shing Wong, the city god, To Tei, the earth god, and Kwun Yum, the Buddhist goddess of mercy. The unit on the far-right is a Shue Yuan, reserved for the community of fortune-tellers. The complex is open daily 8am-6pm, and a small donation is appreciated. Public Square Street is two blocks south of the MTR station, turn right off Nathan Road.

The *Jade Market* is found under the Kansu Street flyover, and can be reached by bus no 9 from Kowloon Star Ferry Bus Terminus, or MTR to Jordan Street. The market has 450 registered stall holders, offering all kinds of jade for all kinds of prices. As mentioned in the Shopping section, this is not the place for buying your first piece of jade, it is for the expert. The market is open daily 10am-3.30pm.

Temple Street becomes a very busy market after 6pm every night, and reaches its peak around 9pm. There are hundreds of stalls stocking a large range of cheap goods, mainly concentrating on menswear. In fact, the old name for the market was Men's Street.

Further along Temple Street, near the Tin Hau Temple area, becomes a street theatre at night, lit by kerosene lamps. There are fortune-tellers and palm-readers, professional chess players, and groups of singers getting into Chinese opera. It is not hard to find - you'll hear it before you see it.

Mong Kok
North of Yau Ma Tei is the district of Mong Kok, which once held the record for the world's most densely populated urban area. Plans to change that have been put into effect, but it is still very crowded.

How To Get There
There is a Tsuen Wan Line MTR station in Mong Kok, or keep walking.

Attractions
Bird Market is in Hong Lok Street, two blocks west of Mong Kok MTR station, and although the last thing you want to try and fit in your suitcase is a bird, a visit is worthwhile. Anyhow, how many bird markets have you been to before? It is to be moved to **Yuen Po Street** where a Bird Garden is set to be contructed

The Chinese have a fascination with birds, and it is interesting to note that the highest prices are not for the best looking birds, but for those who deliver the best songs. We in the west are often accused of pampering our doggies and moggies, but how many of us feed our birds live grasshoppers, and with chopsticks? And, did you know that honey drinks will make a bird sing sweeter?

Ladies' Market, in Tung Choi Street, is the only other attraction Mong Kok has to offer, and it is open every afternoon. Specialties here are jeans, shoes and accessories. The market is two blocks from the eastern Nelson Street exit of Mong Kok MTR station.

Cheung Sha Wan - Mei Foo
Cheung Sha Wan is north of Mong Kok, and the district was developed after the war as an industrial and residential area. Reclamation has removed the 'long sandy bay' that gave the area its name. The new MTR station office and shopping complex highlight the district's plans for modernisation.

How To Get There
There is a Tsuen Wan Line MTR station in Cheung Sha Wan, or take KMB no 2 from Kowloon Star Ferry bus terminal.

Attractions
Lei Cheng Uk Museum in Sham Shui Po, is a branch of the Museum of History, and contains a tomb built during the Han Dynasty (25-220AD), which was discovered in 1955 when a

hillside was levelled for housing estate blocks.

The museum exhibition has full details of the tomb and displays the objects found inside it, which include pottery, bronze pieces, and model houses and barns. The tomb is preserved in situ, in a garden setting protected by a concrete shell and glass viewing wall. It is not known who owned the tomb, but indications are that it was an Imperial Chinese official or settler. The museum is open daily, except Thursday, 10am-1pm and 2-6pm, Sundays and public holidays, 1-6pm. Admission, via a turnstile, is free. Ph 2386 2863.

The Sung Dynasty Village in Mei Foo is most easily reached by KMB no 6A from Kowloon Star Ferry, which terminates at the amusement park next to the Village. The closest MTR station is Mei Foo, which is about 20 minutes' walk from the Village.

The Village is a living museum of lifestyles during Imperial China's Sung Dynasty (960-1279AD), and the 'villagers' are dressed in costumes modelled on those depicted in a famous scroll painting from the period. There is a river with pavilion shops displaying ancient handicrafts, such as calligraphy, incense-stick manufacture, fan-painting, umbrella-making, and candy-making, and visitors can buy some of these products with their special 'Sung money', obtained from the village moneychanger.

In the street there are demonstrations of fortune telling, hawkers, monkey shows, parades, dances and Kung-fu displays. There is also a tea pavilion, a wine tavern and a rich man's house where a wedding ceremony is performed.

The Restaurant of Plentiful Joy serves authentic Sung dishes, accompanied by traditional Chinese folk tunes, and beneath the restaurant is a large wax museum where famous people from China's 5000 years of history are represented. The museum also has a large collection of valuable antiques. All in all, it is a very entertaining and interesting place, and is open daily 10am-8.30pm.

Admission is HK$120 adult, HK$65 child, Mon-Fri, HK$80 adult, HK$35 child, on weekends and public holidays between 12.30pm and 5pm.

Many group tours are available to the Village, and information on these can be obtained from any local tour agent, or from your hotel.

Lai Chi Kok Amusement Park is an informal, old-fashioned entertainment centre next to the Sung Dynasty Village, with rides, dodgems, skating rink, shooting galleries, and, of course, Chinese Opera performances. It is more like a carnival than the modern entertainment centres. Admission is HK$15 adult, HK$10 child, with individual extra charges for the various activities.

The Tsui Museum of Art is about a five minute walk from the Lai Chi Kok MTR station, and has a collection of 2000 pieces of Chinese art including a 500 piece display of ceramics. It is open Mon-Sat 10am-4.30pm and admission is free.

Wong Tai Sin

The district of Wong Tai Sin is named after Hong Kong's most popular Taoist deity, and is home to the HK$3 million temple dedicated to him.

Legend has it that Wong Tai Sin was a shepherd who spent many years meditating and learnt how to refine cinnabar (a mercury ore) into a drug giving immortality. Because of this, worshippers believe the water at the temple has miraculous properties, which is fair, I suppose. But the deity also has a reputation for giving useful tips on the gee-gees (horses), and quite frankly, I don't see how the two things are connected.

How To Get There
Wong Tai Sin is to the east of Mei Foo, on the Kwun Tong MTR Line. It has a station.

Attraction
There is only one - the *Wong Tai Sin Temple*, which is visited by over 3 million worshippers every year. This temple complex is a good example of how the three religions, Buddhism, Taoism and Confucianism can live together.

The Main Temple is a gem of traditional Chinese temple architecture, with red pillars, two-tiered golden roof, blue friezes depicting Taoist, Buddhist and Confucian teachings, yellow lattice-work and multi-coloured carvings.

Offering tables, for fruit, food and lighted joss sticks, line the temple's lower terrace. Taps dispensing the 'miraculous' water are nearby, and fortune-tellers ply their trade to the right of the temple's lower gateways.

The complex also contains the Hall of Buddha of Lighting Lamp, which houses a rock on which the sayings of the Lord Buddha are engraved; the Unicorn Hall, dedicated to Confucius and his 72 disciples, where students pray for high marks in their exams; and the Hall of the Three Saints, dedicated to Hong Kong's three main religions.

The complex is open daily 7am-5pm, and a donation of around HK$1 is gratefully accepted at the entrance.

Kowloon Walled City Park was recently opened on the historic Walled City which contains remains from the Qing Dynasty. It contains flower gardens and a playground. Opened 6.30am-11pm, free admission. It is located on Tung Tau Road off Junction Road. You can alos get Bus 1 from Star Ferry in Tsim Sha Tsui ($4.50). There is a stop opposite the park.

Kwun Tong

To the east of Kwun Tong, the fishing village of Lei Yue Mun is very popular for its seafood restaurants. You can buy fresh seafood from the fishmongers' stalls in the covered alleyways, then take it to a restaurant and have it cooked to your own specifications.

How To Get There
To reach Lei Yue Mun, take the KMB no 14C from Kwun Tong MTR station to Sam Ka Tsuen. From Hong Kong Island, take the cross-harbour ferry service from Sai Wan Ho district to Sam Ka Tsuen.

Attractions
Lei Yue Mun promontory was the point from which the Japanese invasion of Hong Kong Island was launched in December, 1941. For many years after the New Territories lease was signed, Lei Yue Mun was still an isolated shanty community known mainly for its smuggling operations. It has

now been modernised, but maintains an air of antiquity.

The village of Lei Yue Mun has a local sampan ferry service across a small bay. It starts at Sam Ka Tsuen, and takes about two minutes.

Kowloon Country Parks

Lion Rock Country Park is found in the range of hills separating Kowloon from the New Territories. The main peaks are Lion Rock (500m-1640 ft), Beacon Hill (453m-1486 ft), Eagle's Nest (312m-1024 ft) and Mong Fu Shek (255m-837 ft). Wild monkeys are found in the park, and the Eagle's Nest Nature Trail is a gentle 50 minute, 3.2km sign-posted hillside walk, which begins near the Kowloon Hills Country Park Management Centre.

Kam Sham Country Park is known for its Monkey Hills, where bands of long-tailed macaque monkeys live. Section Six of the MacLehose Trail, the most accessible of all the Trail's sections, crosses Kam Shan Country Park. **The 6.4km hike is rated easy**, takes about 90 minutes, and ends near many relics of wartime fortifications.

How To Get There
Take KMB no 81 from Jordan MTR station, or 72 from Sham Shui Po MTR station to the lakelands of the small Kowloon Reservoirs to reach the entrances of both parks. The eastern part of Lion Rock Country Park, and Section Five of the MacLehose Trail, are accessible via Diamond Hill MTR station. From there, take the KMB no 3M service to Tsz Wan Shan housing Estate. Walk on, passing the Kwun Yum temple on the right, then turn right onto Shatin Pass Road and continue straight ahead. This is one of the 18th century stone roads which linked Kowloon with Canton.

The New Territories

The New Territories, or the NT as it is popularly called, is usually regarded as the land beyond the Kowloon Hills stretching to the Shum Chun River, which divides Hong Kong from China's Shenzhen Special Economic Zone.

Parts of the NT seem to have been untouched by modern times, and it is still possible to find villagers and fisherfolk who observe age-old traditions in much the same way as their ancestors in ancient China did.

In amongst these are brand spanking new towns with skyscrapers and modern highways, so it is fair to say that the NT is a land of dramatic contrasts. Also within the area are fourteen country parks and nature reserves.

Visitors who have limited time to spare in Hong Kong would be advised to book on the tour organised by the Hong Kong Tourist Association called *The Land Between*, which will give them a taste of the New Territories.

Tsuen Wan

Tsuen Wan, which means 'shallow bay' was a scattering of villages around a market town when the NT was leased to Britain in 1898. The total population was then around 3000, consisting mostly of Hakka farmers, and the only industry was the production of incense-powder.

Modern Tsuen Wan, which includes the offshore island of Tsing Yi and Kwai Chung container port, is home to almost a million people, but Hakka lifestyles lives on in the hillside hamlets.

How To Get There
The Tsuen Wan MTR station is the terminus of the line of the same name.

Attractions
Sam Tung Uk Museum, on Kwu Uk Lane, is a 2000sqm museum set in a restored 200-year-old walled village. The individual homes have displays of period furniture and exhibitions of

various aspects of Hakka lifestyle, such as festivals, ritual ceremonies and handicrafts. Special exhibitions are found in a hall off the walled village's rear lane. All captions are in Chinese and English, and there is an orientation room where visitors can gain clear insights into ancient lifestyles.

The village is sign-posted from the MTR station, and is open daily, except Tuesday and some public holidays, 9am-4pm. There is no admission fee.

Cheuk Lam Sim Yuen is a 20 minute walk or a short taxi ride from the MTR station, and is one of Hong Kong's most spectacular Buddhist institutions. The 'Bamboo Monastery' was founded in 1927 and has three of the largest 'Precious Buddha' statues in Hong Kong. There is a smaller monastery on the right of the road, and two more on the hill just above.

The *Yuen Yuen Institute*, in Tsuen Wan's Lo Wai village, is a large temple complex dedicated to the three main local religions - Buddhism, Taoism and Confucianism. The main building is a replica of the circular 'Temple of Heaven' which exists in Beijing.

The Institute is a short taxi-ride from Tsuen Wan MTR station, or you can take maxicab no. 81 from Shiu Wo Street, near the station. Vegetarian food is available at the Institute.

The Airport Core Program Exhibition, 401 Castle Peak Road, Ting Kai, ph 2491 9202 houses the engineering exhibition of the projects associated with the building of the new airport. Spectacular view of the bridge linking Lantau Island with the New Territories. Admission free, Open Tues-Fri 10am-5pm, Sat-Sun, 10am-6.30pm.

Country Parks

Tai Mo Shan Country Park surrounds Hong Kong's highest mountain, Tai Mo Shan (957m-3140 ft). The name is Cantonese for 'big misty mountain'. The peak is over an hour's steep hike up surfaced Tai Mo Shan Road, but the views on the way up and at the top are worth it. Near the park's entrance, at the lower level, there is a sign-posted Family Trail, which has good views and is a gentle, 1km, 30 minute hillside walk.

Tai Lam Chung Country Park is a large expanse of hilly

countryside which stretches all the way to Tuen Mun in the north-west corner of the NT. There is only one small village along the whole 22km route of the MacLehose Trail's final two sections. The entrances to Tai Mo Shan and Tai Lam Country Parks are on either side of the road, a few minutes' walk above the village of Chuen Lung. Take bus no 51 from Tsuen Wan Ferry Pier.

Shing Mun Country Park is a 1400ha (3465 acres) lakeland forest, to the east of Tsuen Wan, and surrounding Hong Kong's oldest reservoir, Jubilee Reservoir. There is a local museum in the Park's Visitor Centre, which is near one of the Park's secondary dams, Pineapple Dam. It is open daily, except Tuesday, 9.30am-4.30pm.

This park also contains derelict tunnels on Shing Mun Redoubt, which were laid across the NT in 1937. Visitors should not enter the tunnels.

Section Six of the MacLehose Trail is a scenic 6.4km, 90 minute hill-climb to other attractions, including the Kam Shan Country Park and the Kowloon Reservoirs.

Shing Mun Parks' entrance can be reached by green minibus no 82 from the corner of Shiu Wo Street, near Tsuen Wan MTR station.

Shatin

A self-contained city 11km (7 miles) north of Tsimshatsui, Shatin is close to its targeted population of 700,000. The city has many attractions, including temples, an old walled village, scenic mountain trails, and one of the world's most modern horse racing tracks.

Shatin means 'sandy field', and was settled by Hakka migrants in the 17th century.

How To Get There

Shatin is reached by rail on the KCR. Take the MTR to Kowloon Tong station and change there for the KCR connection to Shatin. The new town has three stations, Tai Wai, Shatin and Fo Tan, with an additional station at the race track.

Kowloon Motor Bus Company services 80M and 81, and the cross-harbour tunnel bus no 170. Travel to Shatin via the Lion Rock Tunnel.

Attractions

The Ten Thousand Buddhas Monastery is the main attraction in Shatin, but be warned - there are more than 400 steps leading up the hillside to the temple. On the way up the hill, in a fenced clearing on the right is the Fat Wah Temple, a Thai-style shrine containing a four-faced Buddha statue. Maybe you will want to pop in here and ask for help with the remaining steps to the top.

The 10,000 Buddhas are stacked on shelves in the main temple, but there are actually more like 13,000, all similar in height, but in a slightly different pose. In front of the temple is a nine-storey pagoda, built to harmonise the temple's *fung shui*, and all around are colourful statues of eighteen of Buddha's followers.

From the pagoda, the views of Shatin are incredible. Below you can see the rail lines heading towards the Lion Rock mountain range above the tunnel, and on the opposite side of the Shatin valley can be seen the profile of the Amah Rock. The rock is on top of a mountain range and get's its name from its shape. Legend says that in ancient times a fisherman's wife climbed the hill, with her baby in a sling on her back, to watch out for her husband's return. She waited day after day, until finally the gods took pity(?) on her and turned her to stone. (Gods like that, you can do without.)

Further up the hill, if you have any breath left, are four more temples, and the one on the far right houses the body of the monastery's founder, a monk called Yuet Kai. After his death, the body apparently refused to decompose, so it was embalmed in gold leaf, and is displayed, ceremonially robed, in a glass case.

The way to the Monastery is sign-posted from the Shatin station.

New Town Plaza is a shopping and recreation centre next to the Shatin KCR station. It has the largest indoor, illuminated, computer-controlled, musical fountain in South-east Asia - amongst shops, etc.

Che Kung Temple is near Tai Wai Village, and is dedicated to a great general from the Sung Dynasty. General Che Kung suppressed a revolt in southern China, and was promoted to a deity after his death. Centuries later, a villager had a dream in which Che Kung suppressed a plague that was then raging in the valley. When the plague ended the villagers built a temple on this site, which has excellent *fung shui*.

Che Kung's festival falls on the third day of the Lunar New Year (late January/early February), and thousands of pilgrims visit this temple then, to pay homage and to turn the bronze prayer-wheel in front of the altar in a clockwise direction to avert bad luck.

Nearby is the *Four-Face Buddha Shrine*, a small statue from Thailand, always decked with flowers. Here devotees pay homage to each face in an anti-clockwise direction.

Tsang Tai Uk, which means 'Tsangs' Big House', is a fortified village built in the 1840s to house members of the Tsang family clan. The builder was a local quarry-master, and the architecture is typical Hakka style of the period. The towers are topped by curved gables at the four corners, and although most of the original windows have been modified, Tsang Tai Uk still retains its traditional rectangular shape incorporating a central courtyard.

Today, the residents are not all members of the Tsang family, as many have moved into the city and their rooms have been rented out.

The village is only a few minutes' walk from Che Kung Temple, via a well-marked subway.

Shatin Racecourse is to the right of Fo Tan railway station, and is one of the most technically sophisticated tracks in the world. It can accommodate over 70,000 spectators, and was built at a cost of HK$60 million. Meetings are held on Saturday or Sunday afternoons during the racing season, September-June, and visitors over the age of 18 can get badges permitting entrance to the Members' Enclosure on presentation of their passport at the betting centre near Star Ferry Concourse on Hong Kong Island, ph 2366 3995. The HKTA's *Come Horseracing* guided tour is available to this track or to the one at Happy Valley, and for further information on the tour phone 2807 6390 Mon-Sat, 28076177 Sun & Public Holidays.

In the centre of the racecourse is a landscaped bird sanctuary called *Penfold Park*, which is open daily, except Mondays, race days and the day following each public holiday.

Tai Po

Now one of the NT's new towns, Tai Po was an ancient market town. It is situated on the banks of the river flowing into Tolo Harbour and so commanded the Imperial trade route between Guangdong and Kowloon peninsula.

The original inhabitants were Tanka boat people, who were conscripted as pearl fishermen a thousand years ago. The pearl trade was so valuable that an Imperial garrison was later established at Tai Po. When the trade died, the troops left, and the Tang clan became Tai Po's dominant power.

How To Get There
The town is serviced by the modern KCR Tai Po Market station.

Attractions
Hong Kong Railway Museum is located in the old Tai Po Market railway station, which opened in 1913. It was built in traditional Chinese style, with ceramic figures decorating the gabled roof-line and brightly painted floral relief murals on the grey-brick walls.

The station's original waiting hall, box office and signal cabin have been fully restored, as have the external decorations. A history of the railway system, including many old photographs of an earlier Tai Po, are presented in an exhibition gallery, and a number of old carriages are lined up beside a covered platform. The museum is open Wed-Mon 9am-4pm, and admission is free.

Man Mo Temple, on Fu Shin Street, is dedicated to the Taoist gods of war and literature. The temple has been restored and inside, on both sides of the main entrance, are two-storeyed 'houses' which were once the town's market management committee rooms and a hostelry for overnight visitors. On the other side of the river, on Ting Kok Road, is another restored temple dedicated to Tin Hau, the goddess of fishermen, but the side hall has altars for the worship of other gods.

Country Parks

Plover Cove Reservoir was completed in 1967 after seven years' work. It took five months to pump out the sea water, and subsequent heightening of the dam has produced a 12 sq km freshwater lake. There are several water sports centres and youth hostels on the sea-water side of the dam. A short walk up Bride's Pool Road is the *Tai Mei Tuk Visitors Centre* (ph 2665 3413), where you can get information and advice on park walks, nature trails and facilities.

Bride's Pool Waterfalls are the most popular attractions on Bride's Pool Road, and are at their best during the summer months. There are two sets of waterfalls, and while neither is particularly big, the settings are scenic. The legend behind the name of the main pool is quite sad. A local village girl was being carried to her wedding in a sedan chair when one of the bearers slipped and the chair was swept over the falls into the pool. The drowned girl was immortalised in the pool and uses the waterfall as a mirror when brushing her hair.

The village of Tai Mei Tuk lies at the junction of Ting Kok and Bride's Pool Roads, and can be reached by the no 75K bus from Tai Po Market KCR station.

Fanling

The area around Fanling has been settled and farmed for many centuries, and the separate villages have now been formed into one large, new town. It is home to nature reserves and the famous Royal Hong Kong Golf Club courses.

How To Get There

By train to Fanling KCR station, or by bus no 70 from Jordan Road bus terminal ($8.00).

Attractions

Luen Wo Market, in Luen Wo Road, is a short taxi ride from Fanling KCR station, and is a typical old-style rural market. Established in 1948, the market was a neutral meeting place for villagers from clans and ethnic groups which had been ancient rivals, and in fact Luen Wo translates as 'united' and 'peace'. The market operates daily 10.30am-noon, and the locals go there to buy fresh produce, but visitors may be interested in picking up a Hakka fringed black hat, or some herbal medicines.

The Royal Hong Kong Golf Club courses at Fanling are among Asia's oldest links, and are named after those of Scotland's St Andrew's. The greens, clubhouse and driving range are open to visitors on weekdays only, except public holidays, and all equipment can be hired. Reservations must be made, and are on a first come, first served basis, ph 2670 1211.

The club is a five minute taxi ride from Fanling KCR station.

Sheung Shui

Sheung Shui is a long-established market town that is now part of the Fanling new town, which has a population target of 220,000. Of the Five Great Clans which migrated to the New Territories' fertile valleys, three - the Haus, Pangs and Lius - are closely associated with Sheung Shui.

How To Get There

Take bus no 68M from Tsuen Wan MTR station to Yuen Long. From there take bus no. 76K to Sheung Shui.

Attractions

Lok Ma Chau Lookout Point offers good views of the Shenzen Economic Zone of China. The lookout has restroom facilities, and there are usually stalls selling souvenirs and snacks. Traditionally dressed Hakka ladies will pose for photographs here, for a fee.

San Tin is the home base for members of the Man clan, who migrated here about five centuries ago. The village of Fan Tin Tsuen, within San Tin, has at least five ancestral halls.

The Man Lun-Fung Hall is thought to have been built at the end of the 16th century in honour of a member of the Man clan. It has been totally restored.

Man Shek Tong Ancestral Hall is one of Hong Kong's finest preserved monuments, and provides a vivid impression of the importance of the Liu clan during the 18th century.

Tai Fu Tai, meaning 'important person's house', was built in

1865 by a senior member of the Man clan, who achieved the highest grade in the Imperial Chinese Civil Service examination. The man obviously did not believe in hiding his light under a bushel, for the house, which is built from granite and traditional grey bricks with colourful terracotta figures inside and out, wood carvings and murals, is flanked by spacious gardens that originally included a lychee orchard.

The house is open daily, except Tuesdays, Christmas Day, Boxing Day, New Year's Day and the first three days of the Lunar New Year. To get there take green maxicab no 75 or 76 from Yuen Long.

Tuen Mun

This is another new town with an ancient history, and the name means 'channel gate'. It was an Imperial outpost guarding the eastern approaches to Deep Bay and the Pearl River estuary. It was attacked and briefly occupied by the Portuguese centuries before the British arrived.

How To Get There

Take bus no. 68X from Jordan Road Ferry Pier to Yuen Long. The 68M bus from Tsuen Wan MTR station also goes to Tuen Mun. The quickest way to get there from Central is by hovercraft from Blake Pier.

Attractions

Ching Chung Koon, meaning 'green pine temple' was originally a rural retreat when it opened in 1949. It is now in the heart of Tuen Mun's high-rise residential area. The temple's gardens are its main attraction, and have pavilions, lotus ponds and a fine bonsai collection. There are also several buildings that are homes for elderly people who wish to spend their retirement in contemplation.

Ching Chung Koon is a Taoist temple dedicated to Lu Sun Young, one of the Eight Immortals of Chinese mythology. The main hall has many treasures, including lanterns from Beijing's Imperial Palace.

Opposite the temple is the Mui Fat Monastery, one of the greatest temples in South-east Asia, decorated with more than 10,000 sculptures of Buddha, and many Chinese and Thai paintings. The entrance is guarded by two spectacular dragons.

Lau Fau Shan, a few kilometres north of Tuen Mun, is well-known for its oyster beds, which cover over 3000ha (7426 acres) of shoreline around the settlement producing gigantic oysters.

Kam Tin

Kam Tin is the original, 10th century settling place of the Tang clan, the first of the Cantonese 'Give Great Clans' to migrate to the New Territories.

How To Get There

A visit to Kam Tin can be combined with one to Tsuen Wan's Sam Tung Uk folk museum: bus no 51 (single-decker) links Tsuen Wan Ferry, south of Tsuen Wan MTR station, with Kam Tin. The no. 64K (single decker) service between Tai Po and Yuen Long passes Kat Hing Wai, as does the no 77K, which links Sheung Shui and Yuen Long.

Attractions

Kat Hing Wai is the best known of the seven walled villages of Kam Tin. Built during the late 1600s, and still inhabited by hundreds of people belonging to the Tang clan, Kat Hing Wai was a monument to the clan's wealth and power, but it was primarily a defensive stronghold against tigers, rival clans, and wandering bands of vanquished Ming Dynasty followers.

The village has been extensively modernised inside, but a moat still surrounds the thick 6m high walls and four corner guardhouse towers with slit windows. The central lane inside the village has souvenir stalls on the way to the temple and ancestral hall, which ruin the atmosphere. There is no entry fee, but donations are expected and a box for them is built into the wall beside the entrance. The pipe-smoking ladies in the Hakka costumes around the entrance are professional photograph posers - it is up to you but I try to ignore them.

Kadoorie Experimental Farm was founded in 1951 by the Kadoorie family, and is on the hillsides on the north-western slopes of Tai Mo Shan, Hong Kong's highest mountain. If you are into agriculture, you have to give two days' advance notice of visiting, ph 2488 1317.

Sai Kung

Situated in the eastern New Territories, Sai Kung peninsula has some of Hong Kong's finest scenery, and some of its most isolated areas. A new golf course with green fees starting at $1000 has been built in the middle of Sai Kung's port shelter, called the Jockey Club Kau Sai Chau Public Golf Course. Sai Kung town is the gateway to a countryside ringed by fjords and wide, sandy bays. Most of the peninsula is contained within the boundaries of Sai Kung East and Sai Kung West Country Parks.

How To Get There

By bus no 92 to Sai Kung from Choi Hung MTR station, or by the no 1 minibus service which stops outside the MTR station near the bus stop.

Attractions

Hebe Haven Marina Cove, which flanks a Sai Kung Port Shelter inlet, is a major, but controlled, property development en route to Sai Kung. There are several supervised beaches which can be reached by foot or local ferries, and the HKTA has all the information.

Sai Kung Town still has back-lane Chinese shops and the harbourside aroma of a fishing community, despite reclamation work and infrastructural developments. The town's temple is, naturally enough, dedicated to Tin Hau, the goddess of fishermen, and is a small complex off Yi Chun Street.

There are several good seafood restaurants specialising in Hakka cuisine, and a surprising number of Western-style restaurants and pubs.

Country Parks

Sai Kung Country Park Visitor Centre has a comprehensive exhibition of maps, relief models, photographs and rural artifacts illustrating the history, geology and natural life of the peninsula. There is also tons of information on the High Island Reservoir project, which enables hikers to enjoy magnificent views by following the first stage of the MacLehose Trail - 10.6km, 3 hours. The centre is open daily, except Tuesdays, 9.30am-4.30pm.

A *Pak Tam Chung Nature Trail* leaflet can also be obtained at the

Visitor Centre. This trail begins a few hundred metres within the park, on a bridge crossing a creek flowing into the Port Shelter. The 30 minute trail has markers enabling walkers to learn about ancient village lifestyles and crops.

One of these markers is by a preserved lime kiln. This local industry was established by a Hakka family in the middle of the 19th century. They built a fortified village with high walls and a watchtower, nearby at Sheung Yiu, meaning 'high kiln'. Their descendants abandoned the village in the 1960s, and later agreed to it being converted into the Sheung Yiu Folk Museum. The terrace of village houses contains typical Hakka furnishings, and galleries provide illustrations, with detailed captions in English and Chinese, of many facets of Hakka lifestyles. The museum is open daily, except Tuesdays and Lunar New Year holidays, 9am-4pm, ph 2792 6365.

The no 94 bus links Sai Kung with the peninsula's two country parks via a scenic coastal road.

Clearwater Bay Peninsula

Clearwater Bay Peninsula is a mountainous stretch of land sheltering the eastern mouth of Victoria Harbour, and the new town development in Junk Bay. Its country park areas are hill-climbers' havens, and its main beach is one of the finest in Hong Kong.

How To Get There
Bus no 91 from Choi Hung MTR station.

Attractions
Clearwater Bay 2nd Beach is the largest beach in the bay and has life savers, changing rooms, snack bars and some children's water slides. Rowing boats can be hired in summer, as the waters within the sheltered bay are generally very smooth.

Clearwater Bay Country Park. Its western part lies to the right of the bay, providing hill walks over Junk Peak. A 30 minute cliff-top walk beyond the bay leads visitors past a picturesque fishing village's cove to the entrance of *Clearwater Bay Golf and Country Club*. Visitors can use the club's facilities, which include an 18-hole championship golf course, tennis courts, restaurants and swimming pool.

Tin Hau Temple in Joss House Bay, is Hong Kong's longest established temple. The bay is normally very peaceful and serene, used only as a drying ground for nets and catches of small fish. But, on the 23rd day of the third lunar month (Tin Hau's birthday), thousands of people flock to the temple.

The original temple was built on Tung Lung Island, to the south-west, in 1012AD, by two brothers who were shipwrecked. This temple was later destroyed by a typhoon, and the brothers' descendants rebuilt it on its present site in 1266. Restorations in 1962 have not destroyed the temple's atmosphere, and it can be reached by a sign-posted walk that begins at the entrance to the Country Club.

Outlying Islands

Hong Kong has 235 islands, but most are uninhabited. Information on the easiest to reach, Cheung Chau, Lamma, Lantau and Peng Chau, is given here, but for the less accessible islands, such as Tap Mun and Po Toi, information can be obtained from the Hong Kong Tourist Association.

The Hong Kong Ferry Co (Holdings) Ltd operates ferry services every day from several piers in Central District, Hong Kong Island, and for schedules, contact the HKTA (ph 2807 6177) or the ferry company (ph 2542 3081).

Following are some HKTA tips for island-hopping:
* Weekend ferries are often very crowded, so it is best to get to the pier at least 20 minutes before scheduled departure times.

* Ferries to Lantau and Cheung Chau operate a deluxe air-conditioned upper deck with a small sitting-out area above the stern. During the week, deluxe supplements can be paid on board, but at weekends tickets for the upper deck must be bought at the ticket office.

* Return tickets are only available for deluxe class. At weekends and holidays, it is advisable to buy return tickets to avoid standing in queues at the other end.

* Ferry services may be suspended at short notice during the summer season (May to October) if a typhoon is imminent.

* Fares start from around HK$6.50 (adult ordinary) and HK$10 (adult de luxe); weekend prices are higher.

What to Take
* *Clothing:* comfortable, casual clothing and shoes are recommended for island exploration; village paths are often steep and narrow and country trails can be rough and mountainous. Take a hat, sunglasses, sun protection lotions, etc, for summer walks.

Maps: for serious explorers and hikers, the detailed Country-side Series No 3 Lantau and Islands Map is recommended. It's on sale at the Government Publications Centre on the ground floor of the General Post Office Building in Central District on Hong Kong Island.

The Lantau Trail guide ($35) is available from the Country Parks Authority, Agriculture and Fisheries Department, 12/F, 393 Canton Road, Kowloon, ph 2688 1111 ext 255, and from HKTA Information and Gift Centres on a supply basis.

General maps of Cheung Chau and Lantau islands can be found on boards by the islands' ferry piers. More detailed Cheung Chau maps are also for sale at local bookshops and holiday flat-rental booths in the village.

Money: small change is useful, especially for Lantau bus fares.

Identification: at all times you should carry some form of identification that includes a photograph.

Tours: guided tours of the islands and daytime cruises are available.

Cheung Chau

Cheung Chau, which means 'long island', is a tiny island 12km (7 miles) west of Hong Kong Island. Although it only has an area of 2.4 sq km (1 sq mile), the population is around 40,000, making Cheung Chau one of the most densely populated of the outlying islands.

It is a popular weekend holiday resort, because of its good ferry service and low rents. There are no cars on the island, so you can walk unhindered through the village's narrow streets.

How To Get There

There is an hourly ferry service leaving from the Outlying Districts Services Pier, and a hovercraft service from the Government Pier on Hong Kong Island. The last ferry from Cheung Chau leaves at 10.30pm.

Attractions

The morning market is one of the island's best sights, and a good place to mingle with the locals. Turn left as you get off the ferry and you will see stalls of vegetables, fruit and flowers, cloth and dried foods, and a display of fish from the night's catch.

Pak Tai Temple is further along the waterfront, behind the playground, where, incidentally, you can hire bicycles for about HK$7 an hour. The temple was built in 1783, and has been recently repainted. It is dedicated to Pak Tai, Supreme Emperor of the Dark Heaven, who legend says defeated the Demon King and his allies, a tortoise and a serpent. Pak Tai has special significance on Cheung Chau as the leading deity in the annual Bun Festival.

Inside the temple there is an iron sword, said to be 1000-years-old, and a 100-years-old wooden sedan chair, which is used to carry the statue of Pak Tai in festival processions. In front of the altar there are large statues of the two generals, Thousand-Li Eye and Favourable Wind Ear, who are said to be able to see or hear anything at any distance.

When leaving the temple, turn right past groups of old folk playing mahjong, and go through the Home for the Aged archway. On the left is a yard where preserved tangerine peel has been made for 80 years.

Tung Wan (East) Beach is situated on the eastern side of the isthmus, about a 10 minute walk from the ferry pier. It is the island's most popular beach, and has life savers on duty April to the end of October 9am-6pm. Further along, past *the Warwick Hotel*, is the smaller *Kwun Yum Wan Beach*, with its tiny white temple dedicated to Kwun Yum, the goddess of mercy. Between the two beaches is a cafe and windsurfing centre.

Cheung Po Tsai Cave is another interesting place to visit, and the best way to get there is to take a kai-do (motorised sampan) from the ferry pier to the Sai Wan pier. Cheung Po-tsai, who was a 19th century pirate said to have commanded a following of 40,000 and a fleet of 600 junks, is thought to have used the cave as a hide-out. He eventually surrendered and helped the government catch other pirates. Near the cave is another temple dedicated to Tin Hau, the queen of heaven and goddess of the sea.

Lamma

The third largest island in the territory, Lamma has an area of 13.5 sq km (5 sq miles), and a population of around 3000, most of whom live in the northern area around Yung Sheu Wan.

It is a mountainous island, with little arable land, and no cars, but it has archaeological importance, being settled in the Neolithic times. However, it's main claim to fame is the dozens of seafood restaurants.

How To Get There

There is a ferry service leaving from Central Harbour Services Pier, the pier before the Outlying District Services Pier. The ferries travel either to Yung Shue Wan, Lamma's main village on the north-west side (every hour and a half), or to Sok Kwu Wan, the village on the east (every three hours).

The last ferry from Yung Shue Wan leaves at 10.35pm, and that from Sok Kwu Wan at 10pm. A kai-do service links Aberdeen to Sok Kwu Wan every 30 minutes, with the last return kai-do leaving Sok Kwu Wan at 6.45pm.

Attractions

Yung Shue Wan (Banyan Bay) has its old market area around Main Street, and the shrimp paste and herbal medicine shops have been joined by modern stores and restaurants, with villas and holiday homes in the hills behind. Bicycles can be rented off Main Street on the way to Hung Shing Ye beach.

Tin Hau Temple is at the end of Main Street, and is over 100-years-old. Two granite lions guard the entrance, and on the inside, behind a red 'spirit screen' (to keep evil spirits from entering) is the main shrine with images of the beaded, veiled Tin Hau. On the left is To Tei, the city god who records important events like births, deaths and marriages, and on the right is Muen Kuen, who guards the temple from evil forces.

The brightly decorated modern shrine in the foothills a little further on is to a local god, the Three Mountain Kingdom King.

One of the easiest, and therefore most popular, walks on the island is between Yung Shue Wan and Sok Kwu Wan, the village in the south. It takes about one hour, following a well-marked concrete path that crosses the barren, eroded mountain top, and continues along the shady coastline.

Sok Kwu Wan, or Picnic Bay, is noted for its many open-air seafood restaurants lining the waterfront. Of course, there is a temple dedicated to Tin Hau, but it has seen better days.

Mount Stenhouse (353m-1158 ft) can be climbed from Sok Kwu Wan. It takes about an hour, and is a surprisingly demanding climb with two really steep sections, so it's not for the unfit.

Beaches
Hung Shing Ye beach, one of the most popular on the island, is about 25 minutes' walk from Yung Shue Wan - follow Main Street from the ferry and turn left before the temple. The beach has changing rooms, showers and toilets, and has life savers during the season.

From Sok Kwu Wan, the best beach is *Lo So Shing*, about 30 minutes away - turn right from the ferry pier and follow the signs to the youth hostel, then turn left for the beach. This beach also has all the necessary amenities.

Mo Tat Wan is a small beach about 25 minutes from Sok Kwu Wan - turn left from the ferry pier - and the village at the back of the beach is about 400-years-old. An occasional kai-do service between Sok Kwu Wan and Aberdeen stops at Mo Tat Wan.

Restaurants
As previously mentioned, Lamma is recognised mainly for its restaurants, and here are a few that are recommended:

Tai Yuen Seafood Shark's Fin Restaurant, 15 First Street, Sok Kwu Wan, ph 2982 8386; *Man Fung Seafood Restaurant*, 5 Main Street, Yung Shue Wan, ph 298 21112; *The Peach Garden Seafood Restaurant*, D.D.. Lot 583, Sok Kwu Wan, 2982 8581.

Lantau
Lantau is the largest island in the territory, with an area of 142 sq km (55 sq miles), and a population of only 25,000. To put this in perspective, Hong Kong Island, which is less than half the size of Lantau, has a population of over 1 million.

With its rugged terrain, undeveloped countryside, peaceful

monasteries and old fishing communities, Lantau is the ideal place to take a break from the hustle and bustle of the city. More than half the island is designated as country parkland, with 70km (43 miles) of well-marked trails, and picnic, camping and barbecue sites. There are also good beaches along the south coast. It development has now proceeded at pace with the building of the new international airport at Chek Lap Kok and the linkage by rail and road to the New Territories by both road bridge and tunnel.

How To Get There

By Mass Transit Commuter Service, Airport Express rail, or taxi that is linked to the New Territories by the Tsing Ma bridge. (Cost from Kowloon to Airport $100 one way). There is an hourly ferry service from the Outlying Districts Services Pier to Mui Wo (Silvermine Bay), with some travelling via Peng Chau Island. A hover ferry service leaves from Government Pier. The last ferry from Mui Wo leaves at 10pm. There are also high speed ferry services operating from Chek Lap Kok Ferry Pier and Tuen Mun in the New Territories at 30 minute intervals. The trip takes about 10 minutes, cost $15 per adult, $10 per child one way.

Attractions

Lantau has buses and taxis, and the bus terminal is near the ferry pier.

Mui Wo, also known as Silvermine Bay, is named after two silver mines that were once in a nearby valley. Its brush with fame came in the 13th century when the Sung Dynasty's boy emperors and their court, fleeing from the Mongols, took refuge here for a time. Today, it is a low-key market town surrounded by new developments, and there are snack stalls and restaurants by the pier, and an old market street across the creek.

Po Lin Monastery is Lantau's most popular sight, and a major centre of Buddhism in Hong Kong. It can be reached by bus no 2 from Mui Wo, and is set amid mountainous scenery on the 520m (1706 ft) Ngong Ping plateau.

The monastery has a large vegetarian restaurant, offers simple accommodation, and many guests who stay overnight rise before dawn to climb Lantau Peak (Phoenix Mountain), the second highest mountain in Hong Kong at 934m (3064 ft).

Established in 1927, Po Lin (Precious Lotus) is a lavish complex, and the largest Buddhist monastery in the territory. The main hall houses the three Buddhas (past, present and future), and the hall below is dedicated to the three Great Beings, who aid the spirits of the dead. The Monastery is also home to the world's tallest outdoor bronze Buddha, constructed in 1990. It is 34m (112 ft), weighs 250 tonnes, and is visible as far away as Macau.

There are several other lesser-known Buddhist monasteries and nunneries on Lantau Island, but only those interested in Buddhism are welcome to visit. If you fit this bill you can get more information from the HKTA.

Lantau Tea Gardens, Hong Kong's only commercial tea plantations, are a few minutes' walk from Po Lin. Here you can sample Wan Mo Cha (the tea of cloud and mist) at a little garden cafe. The Tea Gardens also have horse riding and roller skating facilities.

Tung Chung, on the northern side of the island, is an ancient farming settlement, and the actual site of the refuge of the fleeing princes. Rumour has it that some of the descendants of their followers are still in residence.

A 19th century fort, built as part of an unsuccessful attempt to suppress the opium trade and defend the coastal area from pirates, is about half an hour's walk from Tung Chung. At one time, more than 400 soldiers were stationed here, with five warships in the surrounding waters. Not much of the fort is left now, and the soldiers' places have been taken by primary school children.

Tai O is the largest settlement on Lantau, and is known locally as Little Venice because of the fishermen's houses that are built on stilts in the narrow channel. Most of the town's 6500 residents are descended from Hong Kong's first major settlers, the Yueh tribe.

Tai O was once a garrison town, and the centre for over a hundred years of Hong Kong's salt-panning industry. It is now a quiet fishing village, and most of the salt pans have been converted into fish ponds. Attractions in the town are the rope-drawn sampan which crosses the creek, and the Sun Kit drawbridge at the end of Kat Hing Street.

There are six temples in the vicinity, and two on the island across the creek are interesting. *Kwan Tai Temple* is dedicated to the god of war and righteousness, and was originally built during the Ming Dynasty.

The Hau Wong Temple is at the far end of a causeway overlooking Pearl Bay, and a brass plaque inside tells that the temple was built in 1699 in memory of Marquis Yeung "who rendered meritorious service to the boy emperors of the falling Sung dynasty". It has been renovated recently.

On the opposite side of the creek from the temple is one of Lantau's two stone obelisks, erected in 1902 to mark the boundary with China. Modern surveys have shown that not only are both stones too far to the west, their recorded heights above sea level are way off.

Tai O can be reached by taking the regular no 1 bus from Mui Wo, or bus no 3 from Tung Chung Fort, changing to no 1 at the Tai O bus stop on South Lantau Road.

Beaches
Some of the territory's best beaches are found on a 3km stretch at *Cheung Sha* along the southern coast of Lantau, and at nearby *Pui O*. Cheung Sha and Pui O have life savers on duty April through October, and have toilet and changing facilities, refreshments and accommodation. Bicycles can be hired, and beach camp-sites are available.

Both beaches are accessible from Mui Wo by bus, and get very crowded on the weekends.

The Lantau Trail
A 70km hiking trail, divided into 12 stages of different lengths, links many popular scenic spots on Lantau. For further information, contact the HKTA or the Country Parks Authority, ph 2733 2132.

Peng Chau

Peng Chau is a tiny island to the east of Lantau, and many people pop in for a visit on their way to either Lantau or Cheung Chau.

How To Get There

There are ferry and hover ferry services from the Outlying Districts Services Pier in Central. It takes about 50 minutes by ferry, and 25 minutes by hover ferry ($22 one way), and they run every hour 7am-11.15pm.

Attractions

There is not a lot to see, and the industries that once made the island prosperous have disappeared. The old village and quiet hills make it a pleasant day trip, and there are shops offering hand-painted porcelain, a special local cottage industry.

There is also a 200-year-old Tin Hau Temple almost opposite the pier.

Macau

Macau is linked to China's Guangdong Province by a narrow isthmus, Ferreira do Amaral, and is situated on a tiny peninsula at the mouth of the Pearl River, about 60km (37 miles) from Hong Kong. The territory includes the islands of Taipa and Coloane, to which peninsula Macau is linked by a causeway and a bridge, and its capital is Macau City.

One of the oldest surviving European settlements in Asia, Macau is until December 20, 1999 a Special Territory of Portugal, and has a total area of roughly 16 sq km (6 sq miles), with the peninsula occupying 6 sq km (2 sq miles), Taipa 4 sq km (1.5 sq miles), and Coloane 6 sq km (2.5 sq miles).

History

During the 16th century, Prince Henry the Navigator initiated the great era of Portuguese overseas exploration, and Macau was founded in 1557. It soon became one of the most important centres for trade between Asia and Europe, and attracted the attention of other colonial powers.

The early 17th century saw the Portuguese fighting a drawn-out war of independence against the Spanish, who had control of Portugal. The Dutch thought to take advantage of this and tried on at least five occasions to take Macau, but to no avail, and the territory remained staunchly Portuguese.

The House of Braganza regained control of Portugal from the Spanish Hapsburgs in 1640, and Macau was granted the official title of Cidade do Nome de Dues, de Macau, Nao ha outra mais Leal, which is a very large name for a very small place, and means City of the Name of God, Macau, There is None More Loyal. (It works out to be around 2.6 letters for every square kilometre.)

When the British settled in Hong Kong in 1841, the importance of Macau declined, although it continued to be an important distribution outlet for rice, fish, piece-goods and other Chinese products.

In an effort to encourage tourism, Macau abolished all

customs duties, and legalised gambling, and there is no doubt that the casinos are today one of the main attractions. However, on December 22, 1999, Macau will become a special administrative region of China, although like Hong Kong it will be allowed to control its own affairs for another 50 years.

Climate

The climate for Macau is the same as for Hong Kong.

Population

The total population is around 500,000 and the majority of the people, in fact about 95%, are of Chinese origin. The *Guinness Book of World Records* in 1989, listed Macau as the most populous territory in the world. (Hong Kong was the most populous colony.)

Language

The official language is Portuguese, but don't rush for your phrase book as English is widely spoken, and is the language of trade, commerce and tourism. The majority of the population have Cantonese as their mother tongue.

Religion

After centuries of Portuguese rule, the Catholic influence is strong, although there are only 22,000 of them. Most of the people are Buddhists.

Holidays

Portuguese and Chinese festivals are celebrated, with some religious and most Chinese festivals following the Lunar Calendar, with different dates each year.

Public Holidays are:
January 1 - New Year's Day.
January/February - Chinese New Year.
March/April - Good Friday and Easter Monday.
April 25 - Anniversary of the Portuguese Revolution
May 1 - Labour Day.
June 2 - Corpus Christi.

June 10 - Camoes Day.
June 24 - Feast of St John the Baptist.
August 15 - Assumption.
September - Chinese mid-Autumn Festival.
October 5 - Republic Day.
October 31 - Festival of Ancestors.
November 1 - All Saints' Day.
December 1 - Restoration of Independence.
December 8 - Feast of the Immaculate Conception.
December 24-25 - Christmas.

As with any Chinese community, the most colourful event is the Chinese New Year, and festivities last for about a week.

During the third week in November, Macau hosts the Macau Grand Prix, with drivers and motorcycles, saloon and formula cars coming from all over the world to compete in Asia's foremost motor sports meeting.

Catholic processions which are worth seeing for their spectacle and atmosphere are Our Lord of Passos in February / March, and Our Lady of Fatima on May 13.

Entry Regulations

All visitors must hold a valid passport. Visas are not required by nationals of Australia, Canada, New Zealand, United Kingdom or United States of America, for stays of less than 20 days. Visas can be obtained on arrival if needed. The cost is MOP$100.

Vaccinations are not required, unless entry is via an endemic or infected area.

Apart from drugs and firearms, there are no restrictions on imports into Macau.

Exit Regulations

Macau opened its own International airport in 1995 and so to pay for it there is now a departure tax by air to China M$80, to other destinations M$130.

There are no export duties on any article. However, as travel is invariably through Hong Kong, that territory's import restrictions should be considered.

Also, the Hong Kong Government has levied a tax of HK$26 on passengers embarking to Macau, and Macau has returned the favour by levying a departure tax of M$22 from Macau.

Money

The official unit of currency is the Pataca, which is composed of 100 Avos. Notes are available in 5, 10, 50, 100, 500 and 1000 Patacas, and coins in 1 and 5 Patacas, and 10, 20 and 50 avos. The Pataca is written as M$.

The Macau Pataca is pegged by the Government to the Hong Kong Dollar, which circulates freely in Macau, at the rate of 103.20 Patacas to HK$100.00, with a permissible variation of up to 10%. Apart from small amounts for buses, taxis and admission fees, it is not necessary to change money into Patacas, as you can get away with Hong Kong Dollars. Try not to change any more than HK$20 or HK$30, because **Patacas are not accepted in Hong Kong and any you are stuck with will become just another souvenir.**

Credit cards are widely accepted in hotels and restaurants.

Communications

International Direct Dialling is available, and the country code is 853. International calls can also be made from the General Post Office at Leal Senado Square, Macau City, or Central Post Offices in Taipa and Coloane.

The newspapers are in either Portuguese or Chinese.

Miscellaneous

Local time is GMT + 8 hours.

Electricity in most hotels, the 'New' section of Macau, and the islands is 220 volt/50 cycles. 'Old' Macau has 110 volt/50 cycles. It is best to check before using.

Cotton clothing is recommended for the summer (July-September), but woollens are necessary for the winter (January-March). Sweaters or jackets are sometimes required in the evenings in March-May and September-November.

Travel Information

How to Get There

By Air
Macau's international airport opened in 1995. It is located on the east side of Taipa island. So for travellers making their way to Macau they can come via **Hong Kong or direct from Shanghai, Singapore, Kuala Lumpur and Bangkok. From Europe via Brussels and Lisbon.**

By Helicopter from Hong Kong
East Asia Airlines operate 2 eight-seat Bell 222 helicopters which make the trip in 20 minutes, but the cost is rather high - HK$830 on weekdays, HK$930 on weekends and public holidays. Bookings can be made in Hong Kong at Counter 8, Third Floor, Shun Tak Centre, ph 2859 3359, or in Macau at the ferry terminal office, ph 790 7240.

By Sea

From Chek Lap Kok, Hong Kong
To Shun Tak Centre Terminal, Hong Kong Island: by Airbus no A12 from Departures level, HK$45, 85 minutes; by taxi from Arrivals level, approximately HK$350 (including double tunnel toll, or HK$25), 39 kilometres - so about 60 minutes.

From Hong Kong
There are two facilities for travellers on their way to Macau. The main sea terminal is Shun Tak Centre on the waterfront of Central on Hong Kong Island. It stands over the Sheung Wan station of the MTR. The terminal has booking offices for sailings, reservation office for hotels and an information counter of the Macau Government Tourist Office.

There is another Terminal in Kowloon located at Tsim Sha Tsui alongside Harbour City. It has a booking office.

Jetfoils, operated by Far East Hydrofoil Co Ltd, are the fastest and most convenient. They depart every fifteen minutes in

peak periods and half-hourly at other times, 7am-5pm (winter) 7am-6.30pm (summer), and the journey takes 55-60 minutes.
Fares: M$/HK$142 top deck, M$/HK$129 lower deck (weekdays),
M$/HK$152 top deck, M$/HK$139 lower deck (weekends and public holidays).

A night service (5pm-1.30am, winter, 6.30pm-1.30am summer) is also available, and fares are:
M$/HK$173 top deck, M/HK$159 lower deck (weekdays),
M$/HK$173 top deck, M/HK$159 lower deck (weekends and public holidays.

Bookings: Shun Tak and Macau Terminals or by telephoning 2859 3351, and Ticketmate counters in several MTR stations in Hong Kong up to 28 days in advance, ph 2883 9300.

For credit card (Diners, Mastercard, Visa or Amex) bookings, ph 2859 3333, 2859 6569.

Jumbo, Turbo and Tri-Cats
Operated by CTS Parkview Holding Ltd, take about 75 minutes, and make 28 round trips daily, six from Tsimshatsui, and foru at night.
Fares one way: 1st Class HK$259 weekdays and weekends. Economy HK$129 weekdays, HK$139 weekends and public holidays. Night Service HK$159 weeknights and weekends.

The same company operate *Jumbocats* that take about 60 minutes to complete the journey. They make nine round trips daily. **Fares:** are the same as above.
Bookings: Shun Tak and Macau Ferry terminals, Hotel Grandeur in Macau, and CTS ph 2789 5421 in Hong Kong. You can also use your credit card on this number. Hotline information ph 2851 3533.

HYF Catamarans
Operated by Hong Kong Yaumati Ferry Co. Ltd, ph 2516 9581, depart from Tsimshatsui from 8.30am-5pm and 6.15-9.30pm, and the trip takes 70 minutes. **Fares:** HK$111 (weekday service), HK$128 (weekend day service), HK$148 (night service, both weekdays and weekends).

High Speed Ferries

Operated by HK Hi-Speed Ferries, operate five round trips a day, on Tues, Wed & Thurs, six on Mon & Fri, seven on weekends and public holidays, and the trip takes 90 minutes.

Fares: weekdays - HK$75 1st class, HK$63 2nd class, HK$50 economy class; weekends - HK$86 1st class, HK$74 2nd class, HK$65 economy class.

Bookings: 13th Floor, V. Heun Building, 138 Queen's Road, Central, Hong Kong, ph 2815 3043.

From Kowloon

A limited jetfoil service also operates from the China Hongkong Ferry Terminal in Tsimshatsui, Kowloon. Contact Far East Hydrofoil Co Ltd, ph 2859 3333 for details.

   Note: Except for listed credit card bookings, tickets cannot be reserved by phone. All tickets are for specific sailings.

Ticketmate Bookings

These offices have computerised systems which handle jetfoil, hydrofoil, moke and hotel reservations. They are located in Exchange Square, Connaught Road, Central, on Hong Kong Island, and at MTR station concourses at Tsimshatsui, Jordan, Mongkok, Tsuen Wan, Kwun Tong, Causeway Bay and Wanchai.

Luggage

Jetfoils and hydrofoils have very limited space for large suitcases, so visitors should only carry what they need in Macau. If you have large luggage, it is better to take the ferries. Porters are available at the arrivals wharf in Macau.

NB. The Hong Kong Government charges a departure tax of HK$26 on all travel to Macau, which is usually included in the purchase price.

In Macau
The Macau Ferry Terminal and heliport is at the Outer Harbour near to Yaohan Department Store. It has duty free shops - generally cheaper than Hong Kong duty free outlets, information and booking office.

Tourist Information
The Macau Government Tourist Office in Hong Kong is located at Room 307, Yu Yuet Lai Building, 43-55 Wyndham Street, Central, Hong Kong, ph 2869 7862, fax 2536 4244, and have brochures and all necessary information.

In Macau, the Visitor Information Office at the wharf is open daily 9am-6pm, ph 555 424. The Macau Government Tourist Office, 9 Largo do Senado, ph 315 566, is open during office hours (Web site: www.macau.tourism.gov.mo).

Accommodation
Despite the 4 million visitors who travel to Macau every year, there is usually no trouble finding accommodation, except perhaps during the Chinese New Year holidays and the weekend of the Macau Grand Prix.
Here is a selection, with prices for a double room per night.
Add to the price a 10% service fee and 5% tax.

These prices are in Patacas, but can be read as HK$ if preferred, and should be used as a guide only.

The IDD country code for Macau is 853.
Since bookings are often made from Hong Kong, the relevant local telephone numbers there are given in brackets.

5-star Hotels
Bella Vista, 8-10 Rua do Comendador Kou Ho Neng, ph 965 333 (2881 1668) - 8 rooms, restaurant and bar, transport arrangement - M$1900-4900.

Pousada de Sao Tiago, Avenida da Republica, ph 378 111 (2739 1216) - 23 rooms, restaurants (Portuguese, Continental, Macanese), bar and lounge, coffee shop, swimming pool - M\$1380-1680.

Mandarin Oriental, Avenida da Amizade, close to the wharf, ph 567 888 (2881 1988) - 437 rooms, casino, restaurants (Cantonese, Portuguese), bar and lounge, coffee shop, swimming pool, health club, sauna, squash and tennis courts, free shuttle bus to wharf - M\$1150-1400.

Hyatt Regency Macau, Taipa Island, ph 831 234 (2559 0168) - 346 rooms, casino, restaurants (Cantonese, Macanese, Portuguese), bar and lounge, coffee shop, swimming pool, health club, disco, free shuttle-bus to wharf/Macau airport -M\$990-10000.

Royal, Estrada da Vitoria, at the foot of Guia Hill, ph 552 222 (2543 6426) - 380 rooms, restaurants (Cantonese, European, Japanese), bar and lounge, coffee shop, disco, health club, swimming pool, free shuttle bus to wharf - M\$750-2980.

Hotel Lisboa, Avenida de Amizade, half-way between the wharf and city centre, ph 577 666 (2546 6944) - 1049 rooms, casino, restaurants (Japanese, Cantonese, Chiu Chow, Continental, Portuguese, Shanghainese), swimming pool, disco, casino - M\$900-15000.

Ritz, Rua do Comendador Kou Ho Neng, ph 339 955 (2739 6993) - 162 roms, bar, gym, restaurants, sauna, swimming pool - M\$1180-8880.

The Westin Resort, Estrada de Hac Sa, Coloane Island, ph 871 111 (2083 2015) - 208 rooms, swimming pools, sauna, tennis courts, golf course, shopping arcade, restaurants, child minding services - M\$1625-16000.

4-star Hotels

Beverly Plaza, 70 Avenida do Dr Rodrigo Rodrigues, ph 782 288 (2739 9928) - 300 rooms, restaurant (Western, Chinese, Shanghainese), coffee shop, bar, sauna, shopping arcade - M\$740-1800.

Grandeur, 199 Rua de Pequim, Outer Harbour, ph 781 233 (285 72846) - 338 rooms, restaurants (portuguese, chinese, western), sauna, swimming pool - M\$1000-6050.

Holiday Inn Macau, 82-86 Rua de Pequim, ph 783 333 (free

call 8005646) - 410 rooms, restaurant(have a guess??), bar, swimming pool - M$880-1450.

Nam Yue, Avenida Do Dr Rodrigo Rodrigues, International Centre, ph 726 288 (2559 0708) - 288 rooms, restaurants (western and chinese), children's playground, shopping arcade, coffee shop, business - M$680-3380.

New Century, Avenida Padre Tomas Pereira 889, Taipa Island, ph 831 111 (2581 9863) - 554 rooms, children's playground, kiosk, restaurants (Western, Chinese), fitness centre: squash, tennis, swimming pool - M$1080-2200.

Presidente, 355 Avenida da Amizade, on the waterfront, ph 553 888 (2857 1533) - 318 rooms, restaurants (European, Cantonese, Korean), bar and lounge, coffee shop, disco - M$620-3800.

Pousada de Coloane, Praia de Cheoc Van, Coloane Island, ph 882 143 (no HK number) - 22 rooms, restaurant (Portuguese), swimming pool - M$680-750.

3-star Hotels

Guia, 1-5 Estrada do Engenheiro Trigo, ph 513 888, fax 559 822 - 90 rooms, Chinese restaurants, disco - M$470-570.

Sintra, Avenida Dom Joao IV, ph 710 111 (2546 6944) - 241 rooms, restaurants (European), bar and lounge, coffee shop - M$680-960.

Metropole, 63-63A Avenida da Praia Grande, ph 388 166 (833 9300) - 112 rooms, restaurants (Cantonese, Portuguese) bar and lounge, coffee shop, disco, tour desk - M$460-600.

Mondial, Rua de António Basto, ph 566 866 - 66 rooms (old wing) 75 rooms (new wing), Chinese restaurants, coffee shop - M$400-660.

2-star Hotel

Peninsula, Rua das Lorchas, Ponte Cais 14, ph 318 899 - 123 rooms, along the inner harbour wharves, nighclub and restaurant - M$350-600.

East Asia, Rua da Madeira, 1A, ph 922 433 - 98 rooms, renovated old building, restaurant (chinese and western) - M$230-$450.

1-star Hotel

We suggest you check these out before committing to stay the night though they are recommended by the Macau Government Tourist Office and have english speaking receptionists.

Holiday, Estrada de Repouso 36, ph 361 696 - 40 rooms, no english, M$250.

Kou Va, Rua de Felicidade 71, ph 375 599 - 28 rooms, some shared bathrooms, M$220-$270.

Man Va, Rua da Caldeira 30-32, 3rd,4th and 5th floors, ph 388 656 -Inner harbour, no english, some shared bathrooms - M$250-M$300.

London, Prça de Ponte 4-6, Inner Harbour, ph 937 770 - 46 rooms in decent building - M$250-$400.

Vilas (Guesthouses)
There are dozens of guesthouses known locally as vilas which are usually found on the upper floors of buildings. English is not common and the better ones are similar to 1 star accommodation hotels with ensuite, TV and airconditioning.

Contact the Tourist Office when you arrive to see what they can do for you - ph 510 104.

Local Transport

Buses
There are bus and mini-bus routes in the city, and buses 3, 3A, 10, 12, 28A and 28C provide regular services from the ferry terminal to the city centre. Bus services begin at 7.00am and the last one is around midnight. A single trip within the city costs M$2.50.

There are regular daily buses from Macau City to the islands from 7.00am-11.00pm, and the one-way fares are: to Taipa M$3.60-5.00; to Coloane village M$2.80-4.30; and to Hac Sa Beach M$6.00.

Taxis
Macau has plenty of taxis, painted black with a cream top, and the charges are M$9.00 flag fall and M$1.00 every 1/4 km. Each piece of luggage carried in the trunk costs M$1.00. Additional charges are levied for travel to the islands - Taipa + M$5.00, Coloane + M$10.00, but there is no surcharge for the return trip. Also there is a surcharge of M$5.00 for journeys starting from the International Airport.

From the ferry wharf in Macau to Hotel Lisboa costs

between M$8.50 and M$10.00.

Pedicabs
Unlike those in Hong Kong, pedicab drivers in Macau are quite happy to take passengers for a trip, although don't expect them to be mountain climbers. A tour by pedicab would be an ideal way to see the city, but unfortunately there aren't many drivers with fluent English. Nevertheless, a ride in a pedicab is a lot of fun. The hourly hiring fee, for two passengers, is around M$100, if you find one that can act as a guide, or else try a ride along the Praia Grande Bay which costs around M$25.

Mini-Mokes
Brightly painted mokes are for hire at about HK$500 per day (slightly lower on weekends), with unlimited mileage. Rates are inclusive of vehicle and third party insurance, and drivers must be 21 years of age and hold a valid International Driving Licence. Traffic drives on the right.
For information and bookings contact:
Avis Rent A Car, Shopping Arcade/Car Park, Mandarin Oriental Macau, ph 336 789.
Happy Mokes, Ferry Terminal , level 1, counter 1025 ph 726 868.

The mokes can be picked up at the wharf or airport on arrival, or they will be delivered to your hotel.

Eating Out

Macanese cuisine is a mixture of Portuguese, African, Goanese and Brazilian, with a bit of Chinese thrown in for good measure. The result is, in a word, delicious, and when complemented by an excellent Portuguese wine, makes dining out in Macau a truly memorable occasion.

Considered to be the finest Portuguese restaurant in Macau is the rather expensive by local standards (around M$160-250 for a meal) *Afonso's*, in the Hyatt Regency (ph 831 234), but the oldest is *Fat Siu Lau*, 64 Rua da Felicidade, ph 573 580. It opened in 1903, and is recommended for its roast pigeon, prawn and crab dishes, and much lower prices (around M$75-100). Also in the Hyatt Regency is the *Flamingo* (ph 831234) which offers Macanese and Portuguese dishes, but is even more expensive.

Another of the Portuguese restaurants worth trying is *Pinocchio's*, 4 Rua do Sol, Taipa Island, ph 827 128, which has a garden setting, a budget price range, and specialises in roast quail, chili crab and roast suckling pig.

If you fancy African chicken, a good place to try is *Maxim's Henri's Galley*, 4G-H Avenida da Republica, on the waterfront, ph 556 251. They also serve a great prawn fondu - said to have the biggest prawns in town. A meal costs around M$150.

A popular place with the locals is the *Solmar*, 8-10 Rua da Praia Grande, between the Sintra and Metropole Hotels, ph 574 391. The specialties here are seafood, including a great bacalhau (cod), and African chicken, and they have a good list of Portuguese wines.

For those who only eat when they are hungry, or are in a desperate hurry, *McDonald's* is at 17-19 Rua do Campo, and it's open daily 7am-11.30pm, until midnight on Saturday. You may be surprised at the prices, though.

Attractions

Casinos

The casinos of Macau offer probably the widest range of games in the world, including baccarat, blackjack, roulette, boule, craps, 'big and small', fan-tan, 12 numbers and slot machines, which the locals call 'hungry tigers'.

If you like glamorous surroundings in which to lose your money, the most sophisticated casinos are found in the *Lisboa Tourist Complex*, the *Hyatt Regency Hotel* and the *Macau Oriental Hotel*.

Others, which cater mainly for Chinese patrons, are the *Casino Jai-Alai, in the Jai-Alai Palace; Casino Kam Pek*, on Avenida de Almeida Ribeiro; and the *Floating Casino*, which is moored in the Inner Harbour at Rua das Lorchas near Avenida de Almeida Ribeiro.

All the casinos are operated under government franchise by the Sociedade de Turismo e Diversoes de Macau, and rules are standard in all venues.

Tipping is not expected in the casinos, and if any employee does request a tip, you won't be in any trouble for politely refusing.

This information may come in handy, after you have read the sign that urges you 'not to gamble what you cannot afford' at the entrance to whichever casino you decide to patronise.

Baccarat (or Chemin de Fer)
Minimum bets are M$50, M$100, M$1000, depending on the table. Maximum bet is M$2000, M$60,00 for the table. Maximum payout on any game is M$60,000 for the table.

Blackjack (or Vinte-e-Um)
The casinos operate several kinds of Blackjack tables - some with minimum bets of M$20, others with minimum bets of M$100. The maximum bet on any game is M$1000, or M$3000 depending on the table.

Tokens valued at M$2.50 and M$5 are available from the money change desks for use in this game.

Roulette
The tables in Macau are similar to those found elsewhere in the world. The wheels only carry one zero. The odds on any number from 0 to 36 are 35 to 1.

The minimum bet on any roulette number is M$1 and M$5. Bets of a minimum of M$10 may also be placed on quarter divisions of the wheel, with the exception of 0, which is held by the bank on such bets.

Maximum bets are as follows: single number M$100; two numbers M$200; three numbers follow on a vertical line M$300; four numbers M$400; six consecutive numbers M$100; first, second or third divisions of 12 numbers M$1800; first, second or third column M$1800; colours (black or red) $2500; even or odd $3500; high or low M$3500. Highest payout for the whole game is limited to M$3500.

Players are provided with a chart showing a reproduction of the wheel, the sequence of numbers, the colours and the quarter divisions. It also lists winning numbers from the last few games at the table.

Boule

The main difference between boule and roulette is the use of a large ball on the wheel, which carries a series of indentations rather than the distinct divisions of the roulette wheel.

The 25 numbers on the boule table are also divided into sections to allow a variety of betting combinations.

The minimum bet is M$10. Maximum bets are: single number M$100; two numbers M$200; four numbers M$400; section bearing 4, 6, 8, 10, 15, 17, 19, 21 M$1150; colours (black or red) M$2300; single number bet M$750; single bet on 2 numbers M$2300. Highest payout for the whole game is limited to M$2300.

Fan Tan

This is an ancient Chinese game which uses porcelain buttons. The croupier plungers an inverted cup into a pile of buttons on the table. He then moves the cup to one side. After bets are placed, the cup is lifted and the buttons counted off in groups of 4 until either 1, 2, 3 or 4 buttons are left.

The betting is in cash, which is placed on the table on the numerals 1, 2, 3 or 4; odds or evens; corners; or on divisions between numbers.

Minimum bet is M$20. The highest payout for the whole game is limited to M$3000.

Chipped or broken buttons that may be included in the draw are regarded as valid and will not be discarded. Players are warned not to fold the money, nor to place large currency notes inside small currency.

Big and Small (Sai-Siu)

Another Chinese game based on throwing 3 dice under a covered glass canister. Players place cash bets on the table for dice values, or whether the combined dice will have a 'big' value or a 'small' value.

If the dice all show the same value (for example, all 3s) no player wins, and the banker takes all, unless a player has bet directly on 3 of a kind.

The minimum bet for each game is M$5. The highest payout for the whole game is limited to M$4000.

Slot Machines

These machines are available in a variety of forms in all casinos, and most operate on either M$1 or HK$1. Some accept only HK$1.

12 Numbers

The minimum bet on this game is M$10.

Tombola

Similar to Lotto, Tombola is played Tues, Wed, Thurs and Fri, 8.00-11.30pm, at Jai-Alai Palace on the Outer Harbour, and every Sat, Sun and on Hong Kong public holidays (except Mon) from 3.00-6.30pm at the Mona Lisa Hall in the new wing of the Hotel Lisboa.

Nightlife

Of course, not everyone wants to gamble the night away, some prefer the nightclub scene. Here's a selection of venues available in Macau.

The Crazy Paris Show is a spectacular Las Vegas-type presentation in the Mona Lisa Hall of the Hotel Lisboa's new wing. Show times are: Mon-Fri 8pm and 9.30pm; Sat 8pm, 9.30pm and 11pm; Sun and public holidays 8pm and 9.30pm. Entry is M$120.

Portas do Sol Supper Club on the 2nd floor of the old wing of the Hotel Lisboa has international standard shows and excellent food and wine lists. It is open Mon-Fri 7pm-1am, Sat-Sun 7pm-2am, ph 377 666.

The Hotel Presidente has the *Skylight Disco and Nightclub* on its 2nd floor, ph 553 888, and it is open daily 6pm-4am.

The *Ritz Night Club* is on the top floor of the Jai Alai Palace, ph 726 622, and is open daily 9pm-4am.

A *Karaoke Bar* is located in Basement 1 of the Hotel Royal, and is open daily 8.30pm-2am.

The Mandarin Oriental has its *Bar da Guia* on the ground floor, and it presents live music and dancing; Hotel Guia has a disco nightclub open daily 9pm-4am; and *China City* nightclub is on the 1st floor of the Jai Alai Palace, ph 726 633, open daily 2pm-4am.

Shopping

The main shopping drags are Avenida do Infante D. Henrique and Avenida Almeida Ribeiro, and many people have been known to find bargains in antiques at the flea market in the lanes around Rua das Estalagens, near St Paul's.

The most sought-after items in Macau are gold jewellery, Chinese antiques, porcelain, pottery, watches, electrical goods and knitted wear. All are duty free and no sales tax is charged, but you have to use the bargaining skills that you have honed in Hong Kong.

Make sure that you get a warranty card for jewellery, gold, appliances, etc, and a receipt for all purchases written in a language that you can understand.

Knitted goods and locally-made clothing are very reasonable from the many street stalls near the S. Domingos Market (Senate Square) in the morning, and in Rua da Palha.

Spectator Sports

These sports, in keeping with what seems to be Macau's current reason for being, all involve gambling.

Jai-Alai (Pelota Basca)

This is one of the fastest and oldest ball games in the world. It originated in Spain and requires more skill, stamina and nerve than many other games. But it is easy to understand, and there is a totalisator that takes win and place bets on teams or players at the *Jai Alai Palace*, a 4500 seat stadium directly in front of the main hydrofoil terminal on the Outer Harbour. **Bets range from M$2 to M$250.**

The game is played on a three-walled court, and the players use a wicker racquet, strapped to one arm, to hurl the ball against the sides of the court. **The object is to fling the ball at a wall in such a way that the opponent cannot return it, similar to squash.**

Play begins with a serve by one player who stands about three quarters of the way back in the court. He bounces the ball on the court, catches it in the racquet (cesta) and whips it against the front wall. The ball must rebound to the court between the fault line and the pass line, an area which occupies roughly the second quarter of the court from the front wall. The ball may also be played off the other walls.

The game is played on an elimination basis, with the player who has lost one point retiring to the end of the line-up for the next opportunity to score. **Admission to the Jai Alai Palace is M$2, boxes are M$25 for 6 people.** Bars, snack bars and restaurants are available.

Greyhound Racing

The venue for this is the Canidrome on Avenida General Castelo Branco, and meetings are held on Tues, Thurs and weekends starting at 8.00pm. Admission is M$4 for the public stand, and M$10 for the members' stand. Bar, snack-bars and restaurant facilities are available, and off-course betting shops are located on the ground floor of the Hotel Lisboa, Jai-Alai Palace, and the Kam Pek Casino.

Horse Racing

The Macau Jockey Club holds flat race meetings at the former Raceway of the Trotting Club on Taipa Island. For information on race days, etc, ph 821 188, Taipa.

Motor racing

This event of Formula 3 cars, motor bikes and saloon cars hits Macua's Guia circuit towards the end of November. The circuit of over 3.5 km takes over the city- up over and around the Guia Hill to along the outer harbour. Contact the Macua Tourist office or check the net.

Sightseeing

The Macau Government Tourist Office has an excellent map showing the main points of interest in English, Portuguese and Chinese.

Macau City

Barrier Gate (Portas do Cerco)

Situated at the extreme northern end of the Istmo Ferreira do Amaral, the stucco gateway is crowned by the Portuguese flag. This is the only official crossing point into China, although it is no longer easy to enter Macau at this point, due to the many bureaucratic processes.

Even in years past when the walls of Macau were farther to the south, this point marked the entrance to Portuguese territory. To get there from the city centre, take bus no 5.

Lin Fong Temple

On Avenida do Almirante Lacerda, this temple is entirely Chinese in concept, unlike Kun Iam Tong, which is basically Buddhist. Centuries ago the Chinese mandarins lived in the temple when they visited Macau, and it has altars to many Chinese gods and saints. On the hill behind the temple is the ancient fortress of Mong Ha, but admission is restricted.

Kun Iam Temple

The original temple on this site in Avenida do Coronel Mesquita was probably built more than 600 years ago, but the complex seen today dates from the Ming dynasty, about 400 years ago. Kun Iam is the Goddess of Mercy and Queen of Heaven, and the complex is the largest and wealthiest of Macau's Buddhist temples. Apart from its significance to followers of the Lord Buddha, it also has historical importance for it was here in 1844 that Chinese Viceroy and American Ambassador Caleb Cushing signed the Treaty Wang Sha, which promised 'undying friendship' between the two countries.

The main gate of the complex opens onto a courtyard shaded by banyan trees, and leads to a flights of stone steps, which are guarded by two stone lions, each carved from single pieces of granite, and each holding in its mouth a round stone ball. It is supposed to bring good luck if you turn the balls three times to the left. The locals apparently want to spread good luck - the balls are heavily greased and easy to turn.

The shrines on the right and left, at the top of the stairs, are rarely opened, so proceed through the door in the centre to the main temple. It has three altars on different levels:
the first is dedicated to Buddha and has three gold lacquer images of him behind the altar table;
the second is dedicated to the enlightened Buddha, and there is a gold lacquer image of him behind this altar, enthroned on the Lotus, the symbol of Buddhism;
the third is dedicated to Kun Iam, and her image is dressed in the robes of a Chinese bride.

Along both side walls, in glass cases, there are gold lacquer figures of the eighteen wise men of China, and the one closest to the counter where you can buy 'fortune papers' is of Marco Polo. It is believed that he embraced Buddhism during a stay at the court of the Great Khan. If this is a good likeness, you could say that he was not a very attractive individual.

On the right hand side of the steps going to the main altar, a doorway leads across a lane into a tiny garden surrounding a well of lotus plants and a strange, bent tree. Over several decades this tree has been slowly twisted to form the shape of the Chinese character for 'long life'.

In front of the garden is a small hall of ancestors with tablets recording the life and times of people long gone.

Behind the temple is a large Chinese garden containing several trees, one of which is the subject of an old legend. It is the one that seems to have four separate trunks, and the legend says that two young lovers were forbidden to marry and committed suicide in a love pact. Two trees grew from their graves and joined together in an eternal bond. Consequently it is known as the 'lovers' tree'.

Macau Wine Museum (Museo do Vinho)

Opened in December 1995 the Museum is dedicated to the development of viniculture. In many ways the museum is an expression of the Portuguese culture through wine. In 1400 square metres the Museum presents over 1000 brands, some 300 collectables of which the oldest wine is an 1815 Madeira wine. The museum divides into three areas - History, Cellar/Museum, Wine Exhibition. There are wine tastings and a program of regular events. Rua Luís Gonzaga Gomes, ph 798 4188. Admission is free, M$15 when wine tasting involved. You can get there on Bus numbers 3, 3A, 32 28A, 28C, 10, 10A, 12, 23, 17. It is only a 10 minute walk from the Jet foil terminal.

Macau Grand Prix Museum

The museum shares the same site as the *Museo do Vinho*. Admission here though is M$10. The collection houses cars that have competed in, and won the Macau Grand Prix. Motor bikes, Formula 3 cars and the saloon car divisions feature. A male domain if you don't mind me writing so, and one they will enjoy.

You can get there on Bus numbers 3, 3A, 32 28A, 28C, 10, 10A, 12, 23, 17. It is only a 10 minute walk from the Jet foil terminal.

Macau Maritime Museum

Built at the entrance to the Inner Harbour it's shape is a stylized ship. The old number one wharf has been incorporated into the building. It is a celebration of Macau's involvement with the sea from featuring the legend of the sea goddess A-Ma to Portugese exploration. It has three levels, the first is dedicated to fishing themes, the second level focuses on great voyages of discovery from primitive vessels to the time of Prince Henry the navigator. The third level displays mockups of vessels used in transport to the present day. The Museum also houses an aquarium and has outdoor exhibits some of which are interactive. You tend to see the dad's playing with these rather than the kids. Opened 10.00am to 5.30pm. Closed on Tuesdays. Admission M$8 adults, M$4 child. Sunday is cheaper.

Guia Fort (Fortress of Our Lady of Guia)

Built between 1637 and 1638 on the highest point of Macau, the fort occupies around 800 sqm (8600 sq ft) in the shape of a rough pentagon. The walls are of masonry and rise about 3m (10 ft), and two of the original brickwork turrets remain.

The fort was built to defend the border with China, but because of its position overlooking the entire city, its main function was as an observation post. It had a barracks, a water cistern, ammunition and equipment stores, the commander's

house, and a hermitage dedicated to Our Lady of Guia.

In 1865, a lighthouse was added, and it is the oldest on the China coast. The light can be seen for 20 miles in clear weather, and was electrified in 1909. Near the lighthouse is a post where signals are hoisted to warn of an approaching typhoon. Before it was erected, storm warnings were announced from the bell-tower of the hermitage.

At the entrance to the chapel, which is only open on August 15, its saint's day, is a grave-stone with a Portuguese inscription. The translation is *"Here lies at this gate the remains of Christopher, by accident, for his body does not deserve such an honourable sepulchre"*. Sounds like there could be an interesting story behind that, but no-one knows who Christopher was, or what he did.

There are restroom facilities and an information counter. You have to walk to the fort, which is open 7am to sunset.

Memorial House of Sun Yat Sen
Dr Sun Yat Sen, the founder of the modern Chinese Republic, practised medicine in Macau for some time prior to the otherthrow of the Ching Dynasty of the Manchu Emperors on the mainland in 1910. The house in Avenida Sidonio Pais, near the police station, was built by his family to house his relics. It is open Mon, Wed, Thurs & Fri 10am-1pm, Sat & Sun 3-5pm.

Lou Lim Ieoc Garden
The garden was built in the 19th century by a wealthy merchant, and is modelled on the gardens in Soochow. It is a pleasant place to while away a half hour or so.

Monte Fort (Fortress of Sao Paulo do Monte)
Situated almost in the centre of Macau in a public park, the fort is reached by a narrow cobblestone street, and is closed between dusk and dawn. It was built by the Jesuits about the same time as St Paul's. The Fort was the central point of the old city wall that stretched west to the village of Patane, and east to Sao Francisco Fort on the northern headland of the Bay of Praia Grande.

There is a story that the Jesuits lost the fortress when an early governor invited himself to dinner, and when the hosts hinted that it was time to call it a night, the governor and his bodyguards 'convinced' the Jesuits to evacuate.

The main event in the fort's history occurred in 1622 when the Dutch attempted to invade Macau. On June 24, the feast day of St John the Baptist, a defending cannon ball from the fort's guns landed in the Dutch magazine and put paid to the Dutch attack. St John was immediately acclaimed as the patron saint of the city.

Today the fort contains the Weather Observatory, and in the far north-eastern corner there is a collection of ancient carved stones dating back to the earliest days of Macau.

It's a great place to get views of the city and the adjacent Zhongshan district.

Refreshments and restroom facilities are available, and on the weekends and public holidays, students dressed in 18th century uniforms parade around the main entrance.

The Ruins of St Paul's

The most famous sight in Macau is the ruined facade and steps of the Church of the Mother of God, popularly known as St Paul's. It was built adjoining the Jesuit College of St Paul's, the first Western college in the Far East, and a cornerstone dates its construction to 1602. According to early travellers, it was built of taipa and wood, and brilliantly furnished and decorated. The carved stone facade and staircase were added in 1620-27 by Japanese Christian artisans who had fled from persecution in Nagasaki, under the direction of Italian Jesuit Carlo Spinola. When completed the Church was described as "the greatest

monument to Christianity in all the Eastern lands" and the crowned heads of Europe vied with each other to present the church with ornate gifts. After the Jesuits were expelled, the college was used as an army barracks, and in 1853, a fire started in the kitchens and destroyed the college and the body of the church.

The facade rises in four colonnaded tiers, and is covered with carvings and statues that illustrate the early days of the Church in Asia. They include statues of the Virgin and saints, symbols of the Garden of Eden and the Crucifixion, angels and the devil, a Chinese dragon and a Japanese chrysanthemum, a Portuguese sailing ship, and various pious warnings inscribed in Chinese.

St Anthony's Church

St Anthony's, in Rua de Sao Antonio, is built on the site of a chapel founded in 1558, the first to be built in Macau. The present church has had a series of mishaps, according to a plaque by the door, which says: "Built in 1638. Burnt in 1809. Rebuilt in 1810. Burnt again in 1874. Repaired in 1875." It could go on to say, "Burnt and restored in 1930. Restored in 1940.".

St Anthony is a 'military' saint, and a 'captain' in the Portuguese army. Each year on June 13 (his feast day) the President of the Senate presents him with his wages. A statue of him is taken to inspect what is left of the old city battlements.

Old Protestant Cemetery

A marble plaque over the door to the Cemetery is inscribed "East India Company, Old Protestant Cemetery 1814", but many of the graves predate the plaque. It was several decades after the arrival of Protestant traders that the East India Company bought the land for use as a cemetery, so many of the older graves outside the city wall were re-interred here.

Inside the entrance is a small Anglican Chapel, where English-language services are still conducted every Sunday. A sloping paths then leads to the cemetery, which was restored with the assistance of noted historian Sir Lindsay Ride whose ashes were interred here in 1978.

The cemetery is on two levels, and the smaller upper tier leads to the grave of the well-known China coast artist George Chinnery. The larger lower level has the graves of seamen and traders from many nations, and a few famous people, including Dr Robert Morrison, who compiled the first English/Chinese dictionary and translated the Bible into Chinese, and Captain Lord John Spencer Churchill, an ancestor of Sir Winston.

Luis de Camoes Museum

Situated between the Old Protestant Cemetery and the Camoes Garden, on the Praca Luis de Camoes, the museum is named after Portugal's most famous poet. It dates from 1770, and was once the headquarters of the select committee of the British East India Company. The museum has a superb collection of artistic and historic paintings. It is open Thurs-Tues 11am-5pm.

Leal Senado

The 'Loyal Senate' faces the main civic square of Macau on Avenida Almeida Ribeiro, and the building is regarded as the best example of traditional Portuguese architecture in the territory. The Leal Senado had enormous power and influence in the early days of Macau, but it now functions as the Municipal Council. The building has been restored and is worth a visit. It also houses the Public Library.

The Cathedral

The present building in Largo da Se is on the site of several previous cathedrals. The original was the Church of Our Lady of Hope of St Lazarus, declared the mother church of the Macau Diocese, which included the religious provinces of China, Japan, Korea and other islands adjacent to China.

The first stone Cathedral was consecrated in 1850, and almost destroyed in a typhoon in 1874. It was completely rebuilt in 1937, and has two solid towers and massive doors. The stained glass windows are particularly beautiful.

Other churches were are worth visiting are: St Dominic's in Rua de Sao Domingos; St Augustine's on the Largo de Sao Agostinho; St Lawrence's in Rua de Sao Lourenco; and the Seminary Church of St Joseph, which has only been open to the public since March 1990 (daily, except Wed, 10am-4pm).

Taipa

Taipa village is known for its fireworks and textile factories, the

United Chinese Cemetery, the University of East Asia, and the *Taipa Folk Museum*.

The Museum consists of five colonial-style mansions designed to show how Portuguese families lived at the turn of the century. They have large interiors featuring dining and living rooms, ball rooms, halls for games and playing cards, kitchens, and large verandahs that face the sea through an avenue of old banyan trees. They are furnished in the style of the period. The museum is open Tues-Sun 9.30am-1pm, 3-5.30pm.

The Church of Our Lady of Carmel, which was built in 1885, stands on a hill overlooking the village and museum.

Coloane

The island of Coloane attracts most visitors because of its beaches and its greenery. Coloane village has an interesting Chinese temple, and a junk-building yard.

Chapel of St Francis Xavier

South of the village is the cream and white Chapel of St Francis Xavier, which contains some of the most sacred relics of Christian Asia.

Persecution of Christians in Japan led to twenty-six foreign and Japanese Catholic priests being crucified in Nagasaki in 1597, and many hundreds of Christian Japanese were killed during the 1637 Shimabara Rebellion. The bones of the Martyrs and some of the rebels were brought to Macau, and kept in St Paul's. After it was destroyed the bones were taken to the Cathedral, then moved to St Francis Xavier Chapel in 1974. St Francis Xavier died on Sanchuan Island, 50 miles from Macau in 1552, and a bone from his right arm is preserved in the chapel.

Coloane Park
North of the village is Coloane Park, built on the 20ha (50 acres) site of the former Agriculture and Forestry Department's gardens. It has extensive gardens and ponds, a large walk-in aviary, and an air-conditioned display room of local flora and fauna. The park is open daily 9am-7pm, and is reached by taking bus 21 or 21A from opposite the Hotel Lisboa.

Cheoc Van
This is Macau's most popular beach, and is home to the Macau Yacht Club and Cheoc Van Pool, a complex consisting of an irregular shaped swimming pool,a restaurant-bar and changing rooms. The pool is open daily 9am-10pm, and the beach has life savers on duty throughout the summer.

Hac Sa
Another popular beach, which is patrolled during the summer, Hac Sa means 'black sands'. Behind the beach is the Hac Sa Sports and Recreation Complex, which covers nearly 1.8ha (4.5 acres) of land and has an Olympic-size swimming pool, a kiddies' pool, roller skating rink, sports field, facilities for tennis, basketball, mini-soccer, mini-golf, and picnic and barbecue facilities. The complex is open daily 9am-10pm.

Ka Ho
Also known as Pirate's Bay, Ka Ho is situated at the northern end of the island, and was a haven for pirates in days gone by. Now it is a tiny farming community.

Tours
Tour operators are licensed in Macau, and are under the supervision of the Macau Government Tourist Office. It is strongly recommended that you never use the services of an operator who is not licensed, because there is probably a good reason for the absence of a license.

City Tour

Usually lasting 3 to 3.5 hours, the tour includes Barrier Gate, Kun Iam Temple, Ruins of St Paul's, Sun Yat Sen Memorial Home, Guia Circuit, Lou Lim Ieoc Garden, Penha Church and Bishop's Residence, Leal Senado, Floating Casino, and Jai-Alai Stadium.

Costs per person:
by air-conditioned coach - M$70;
by limousine - M$175.
These prices included a meal with a glass of wine.

Islands Tour

Usually lasting 1.5 to 2 hours, the tour includes the Harbour Bridge, Macau Jockey Club, Taipa Village, Temple of Kun Iam, Junk-building village, Coloane town, St Francis Xavier's Chapel, Tam Kong Temple, Cheoc Van Resort, Hac Sa village and beach.

Costs per person: by air-conditioned coach - M$25.

Budget Tour

Sintra Tours offer a highlights tour using a tape recorded commentary. It starts and ends at Hotel Sintra, and lasts 2.5 hours. The itinerary includes Penha Church and Bishop's Residence, Barrier Gate, Kun Iam Temple, Sun Yat Sen Memorial Home, and the ruins of St Paul's.

Costs per person: M$30, with a minimum of 10 persons.
The tour is available at weekends and on Hong Kong holidays.

Tour Machine

A fleet of replica English buses of the 1920s, equipped with air-conditioning and seating up to 9 passengers, operates on fixed routes with stops at significant attractions along the way. These explorer-type tours cost M$25-50 on the city route and M$30 on the islands route.

For reservations contact the Macau Tourist Office, or book at the Tour Machine kiosk in front of Hotel Lisboa, where the tours begin and end.

Harbour Cruise

The Maritime Museum operates a special cultural tour of the Inner Harbour each Sat, Sun, Mon and public holiday. The vessel is a specially-converted fishing junk, and recorded tapes in English, Chinese and Portuguese give details of the customs and life of local fishermen.

The cruise lasts 40 minutes, leaves from Pier No. 1 in front of A-Ma Temple at 10.30am, 11.30am and 3pm.

Costs M$30 adults, children under 12 free.

Tickets can be purchased at the Pier No. 1 counter, ph 595 481.

The Macau Watertours offer a variety of cruises at the same pier, daily 9.30am-5pm. There are choices ranging from 30 minutes to 1.5 hours, and the prices start from M$50 for adults.

Index of Maps

Index

Macau